Easy PC
web site
construction

Other Computer Titles

by

Robert Penfold

BP470   Linux for Windows users
BP484   Easy PC Troubleshooting
BP495   Easy Windows Troubleshooting
BP503   Using Dreamweaver 4
BP504   Using Flash 5
BP507   Easy Internet Troubleshooting
BP518   Easy PC Peripherals Troubleshooting
BP521   Easy Windows XP Troubleshooting
BP523   Easy PC Interfacing
BP527   Using Flash MX
BP530   Using Dreamweaver MX
BP531   Easy PC Upgrading
BP534   Build Your Own PC
BP536   Using Photoshop 7
BP537   Digital photography with your computer
BP540   Easy PC Security and Safety
BP541   Boost Your PC's Performance
BP542   Easy PC Case Modding
BP549   Easy PC Wi-Fi Networking

Easy PC web site construction

Robert Penfold

Bernard Babani (publishing) Ltd
The Grampians
Shepherds Bush Road
London W6 7NF
England
www.babanibooks.com

Please note

Although every care has been taken with the production of this book to ensure that any projects, designs, modifications and/or programs, etc., contained herewith, operate in a correct and safe manner and also that any components specified are normally available in Great Britain, the Publishers and Author do not accept responsibility in any way for the failure (including fault in design) of any projects, design, modification or program to work correctly or to cause damage to any equipment that it may be connected to or used in conjunction with, or in respect of any other damage or injury that may be caused, nor do the Publishers accept responsibility in any way for the failure to obtain specified components.

Notice is also given that if any equipment that is still under warranty is modified in any way or used or connected with home-built equipment then that warranty may be void.

© 2003 BERNARD BABANI (publishing) LTD

First published – September 2003
Reprinted – July 2004

British Library Cataloguing in Publication Data

A catalogue record for this book is available from the British Library

ISBN 0 85934 539 4

Cover Design by Gregor Arthur

Printed and bound in Great Britain by Cox & Wyman Ltd, Reading

Preface

Not so long ago you needed to be a techie type in order to view web pages, and a hardcore techie or professional in order to produce web sites. These days the situation is very different, and all but the worst of technophobes can surf the net. You no longer need to be an expert HTML programmer in order to produce a site and publish it on the Internet. Provided you have some experience of using a computer and the Internet it is possible to produce a simple site and upload it to a server in an hour or two. If you already have the source material prepared then it could probably be done in a matter of minutes.

With modern WYSIWYG (what you see is what you get) web page creation programs you can produce quite complex pages and sites without any knowledge of HTML at all. The cost of having your own web site can be surprisingly low. Apart from the costs of the electricity to run your PC and any Internet connection charges, it can cost precisely nothing to produce, upload and run a site. You are not limited to simple sites either. You may well have been assigned 20 to 100 megabytes of free web space when you signed up with your Internet service provider. This is sufficient for a substantial web site. There is plenty of free or cheap web space on offer from numerous companies.

Once you know how, it is easy to construct and upload your site, and this book shows you how. A number of different approaches are covered. It is possible to produce very professional looking sites using certain programs that are not specifically designed for producing web pages. Microsoft's Word is perhaps the most common example of a program of this type. You may already be using software that is suitable for producing web sites. Another option is to use a free web page creation program such as Netscape Composer. If you are prepared to spend a modest amount of money it is possible to obtain a professional-quality site creation program such as Netobjects Fusion. A fourth, and increasingly popular approach, is to build the site online using the facilities provided by the web host, or web publishing as it has become known.

Whether you wish to produce a personal or family site to keep friends and family members in touch, a hobby site to promote your favourite pastime, or a site to help publicise a small business, the methods described here will make things as quick and easy as possible. The reader is not assumed to have any previous knowledge of HTML or web site construction, but it is assumed that he or she knows the basics of using a PC and using the Internet.

Robert Penfold

Trademarks

Microsoft, Windows, Windows XP, Windows Me, Windows 98 and Windows 95 are either registered trademarks or trademarks of Microsoft Corporation. Photoshop and PageMaker are registered trademarks of Adobe Systems Inc.

All other brand and product names used in this book are recognised trademarks, or registered trademarks of their respective companies. There is no intent to use any trademarks generically and readers should investigate ownership of a trademark before using it for any purpose.

Contents

1

Basic elements 1

The basics 1
Types of site 1
Personal 2
Family site 2
Small Business 2
Large business..3
Online business 4
Fan/hobby sites 5
Multi-channel..6
HTML 6
Roundtrip HTML 7
Mark-up 8
HTML basics..8
Tags 11
Why use HTML? 11
File types 12
Jpeg or Jpg 12
GIF 13
Png 13
Txt 14
Other formats 14
Aif or Aiff...14
AVI 15
Mpeg or Mpg 15
Mov 15
Swf 15
PDF 15
MP3 16
WMA and WMV 16
MIDI 16
DHTML 16
JavaScript..16
CSS 17
DOM 17

XML 17
Page elements 17
CGI, etc. 18
Entering text 19
Headings 20
Lines and lists 22
Tables 23
Padding and spacing 26
Frames 26
Framesets 28
Adding links 31
Relative links 31
Relocating 32
Hot spots 35
Named anchors 37
Linking files 40
Multimedia 44
Software 45
WYSIWYG 48
Uploading 50
Points to remember 53

2

Design matters 55

Look and learn 55
Grand tour 55
Purpose 56
Minimalism 57
Colour conscious 59
Consistent approach 61
Text size 62
Fonts 62
Headings 63
Hyperlinks 64
Missing link 67
Music 69

Images 69
Download time 70
Pop-ups 71
Missing material 72
Spelling 73
Style 74
Under construction 77
Clear idea 78
Templates 79
Wizards 80
Points to remember 84

3

Hosts and web publishing 87

Options 87
Free 87
Free drawbacks 88
Down time 89
Facilities 90
ISP hosting 91
Hired space 92
Free choice 94
Web Publishing 96
Preview 103
Editing 107
Second page 108
From scratch 114
Text 118
Text colour 119
Rollover 121
Link text 121
Backgrounds 123
Add-ons 127
Menus 129
Aligning objects 131
Other tools 131

Photo albums 134
Adding photographs 137
Image editing 141
Finally 147
Points to remember 149

4

Web graphics 151

Pixels 151
Detail 153
Why process? 156
Compression 157
Pick of the crop 160
Feathering 165
Downsizing 166
Controlling compression 170
Sharpening 173
Unsharp Mask 177
Background image 180
Generating backgrounds 182
Indexed Color 188
File conversion 191
GIF 191
Png 192
Large text 193
Finally 195
Points to remember 196

5

Web creation software 199

Word processor 199
Pictures 203
Tables 209
Web wizard 213

The real thing 218
HTML export 221
Netscape Composer 222
Basic tables 225
Adding an image 229
Dialogue boxes 232
Anchors and links 235
Fusion 241
Page style 244
Adding content 246
Adding images 249
Photo gallery 254
Testing 256
FrontPage 262
Web site templates 265
Photo albums 270
Points to remember 273

6

Uploading and promotion 275

Integral upload 275
FTP program 282
File management 286
Browser upload 288
Fault-finding 290
Relativity 291
Missing homepage 292
Missing FrontPage 292
Filenames 293
What site? 294
Yahoo! 297
Paying up 299
Showing up 300
Registration URLs 302
Points to remember 303
Index 305

Basic
elements

The basics

Presumably you already have some knowledge of web sites and surfing the Internet. If not, then the next step is to get online and look at some web sites, and learn a few fundamentals of the Internet. Even if you do have some Internet experience, it would probably still be a good idea to go online and study some web sites of various types. Look at the content of some web pages, and I do not mean just read the main text and look at the pictures. Look at everything on each page. There are page headings, subheadings, links to other sites or other pages within the same site, pictures, blocks of text, and text that appears when the pointer is placed over many of these elements.

These are the basic elements you will use when building your own site. Some sites have clever features such as animations, sound, and rollovers (pictures that change when the pointer is placed over them). This type of thing is optional, and in general it is best to use the clever tricks sparingly. What is intended to make a site more lively can easily end up being an irritation that makes users leave the site. Slow moving animations of poor quality are more or less guaranteed to drive users away from your site.

Types of site

Early in the proceedings you need to decide on the type of site you require. Some types of site are easily produced in a less than an hour with little or no previous experience of web site construction. Other types of site require hundreds or even thousands of man-hours and huge amounts of expertise. Most sites fall somewhere between these two extremes. Using modern software it is possible for beginners to produce some quite complex web sites, but there is a limit to how far you can reasonably expect to go with your first attempt. If you need a really complex site you will either have to gradually build up to it or get in a professional site designer from the start.

Although there are numerous types of site, most fall into one of these broad categories:

Personal

This is a site about you that contains whatever you wish to tell the world about yourself. Typically there is at least one photograph of you, together with details of where you live, your hobbies, etc. Sites of this type are primarily for family and friends. Provided the site is kept up to date, a family member living on the other side of the world can log onto your site from time to time to see how you are doing. Do not expect mass traffic on this type of site. Unless you are famous or share the same name as someone famous, few people will stumble across your site and even fewer will stay long.

Family site

Much the same as a personal site, but covering the whole family. Again, this type of site is only likely to be of interest to your family and friends. Personal and family sites are easily built by non-professionals and can usually be put together quite quickly.

Small business

The term "small business" is a bit vague, since in some contexts companies worth a hundred million pounds or more are considered to be small. Here we are really talking in terms of anything from a one-man business to a company that has perhaps a dozen or so employees. In fact quite large companies can have this type of site, since a large company does not necessarily need a huge web site. For example, manufacturers that do not deal direct with the general public often have quite modest web sites. The site typically has some product information and a list of authorised dealers. Any online ordering facilities will be provided by the dealers.

The contents of the site will obviously vary considerably depending on the nature of the business. A site promoting an artist would include a brief biography of the artist and some photographs showing examples of his or her work. There would also be details of any upcoming exhibitions, opening times of the studio shop, and so on. A site for a

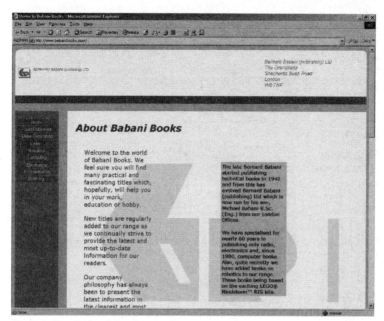

Fig.1.1 The Babani Books site is a good example of a business site

larger business would typically have a brief history of the company, details of its products or services, where to buy the products, and so on. The Babani Books site (www.babanibooks.com) is an example of a site in this category. Figure 1.1 shows the Babani homepage.

Many small business sites are produced by professionals. This is not to say that building this type of site is beyond the scope of a beginner. However, it is essential to take the task seriously and put in as much time and effort as it requires to do the job properly. A poorly designed site is not going to be a good advertisement for your company, and could even be counterproductive. It is more than a little helpful to have some natural design ability, but you can always copy the general scheme of things used in a similar site if your design skills are practically non-existent.

Large business

As already pointed out, a large business site is not necessarily that much different to one for a smaller company. It is almost certain to be produced professionally though, either by in-house specialists or outside

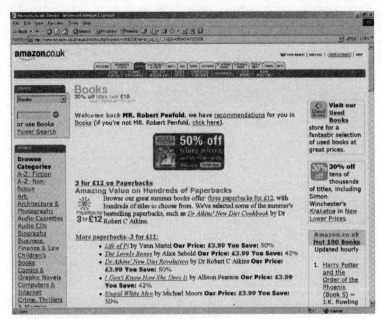

Fig.1.2 Amazon is probably the best known online retailer. This is the homepage of their UK site

contractors. Consequently, this type of site is ideal if you are looking for design ideas and general guidance on laying out pages or a complete site.

Online business

Strictly speaking an online business is one that only operates via the Internet, but many of these sites are actually owned by large retailers that have shops and (or) conventional mail order businesses. Amazon (Figure 1.2) is probably the largest and best known of the true e-tailers. Even a relatively small online business is likely to require a complex site since there will usually be online ordering facilities in addition to all the normal product information, etc. There are programs that can help you to produce your own online shop, and some web space providers have a facility of this type provided as part of an e-tailing package. Setting up this type of site is more complicated than putting together a normal site though, and it goes beyond the scope of this book.

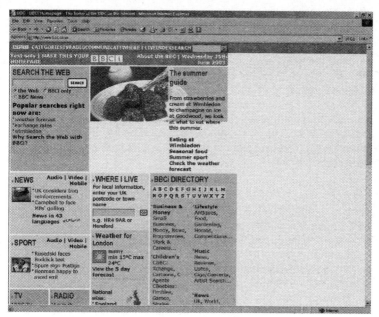

Fig.1.3 The BBCi is the UK's biggest multi-channel site

Fan/hobby sites

Some of these are commercial sites, but many of them are run by individuals or small groups at their own cost. These generally have articles about the hobby, football team, or whatever, plus all the latest news about the subject of the site. This type of site is relatively easy to construct and should not be beyond the capabilities of most beginners. With fan sites it is important to make sure that nothing is included on the site unless you own the copyright or have permission to include it. Many fan sites have been threatened with legal action for including pirated material such as audio/video clips or photographs.

Never include anything on a web site unless you own the rights to it or have permission to do so. The only exceptions are things that are in the public domain. In other words, material where the copyright has lapsed or the owner has decided not to claim copyright in the work. You can buy CDs of royalty-free photographs and music for example, and there should be no problems in using this type of material on your site.

Multi-channel

A multi-channel site is simply one that covers a wide range of subjects. It is effectively several sites accessed via one address and homepage. Probably the best known and biggest multi-channel site in the UK is the BBCi site (Figure 1.3). Yahoo! is probably the best known international multi-channel site. In theory it is perfectly possible to produce your own multi-channel site, and having everything at one web address is likely to be much cheaper than using a different address and site for each topic. In practice it could be quite difficult and time consuming setting up a site that covers several subjects in reasonable detail. It is probably not a good starting point.

HTML

Web pages are written using what could be regarded as a form of programming language, known as HTML (hypertext mark-up language). As its name suggests, it is actually more like a mark-up language used in a desktop publishing program than a true programming language. Those of us that can remember desktop publishing in the days before that term had been invented can also remember the relatively crude way in which pages were produced. There were no true WYSIWYG (what you see is what you get) desktop publishing programs for the early PCs and other computers of that era. Instead, embedded codes were used to indicate that pieces of text should be in a certain font, style, and size.

What appeared on the monitor was the text plus the embedded codes in the standard font of the computer's video card. This was usually a pretty crude monospaced font, and the monitor often gave little idea of the page's true appearance. In order to see what a page looked like you had to print it out. If there were any problems or you simply did not like some aspect of the page design, the embedded codes had to be changed and then the page was printed out again. This sounds like slow and tough going, and it was.

Modern desktop publishing programs do not work on this basis, and the monitor does provide something close to a true WYSIWYG display. The resolution of even a good monitor is usually well below the final printed resolution, requiring some compromises to be made in the version displayed on the monitor. Nevertheless, you get a very good idea of what the final printed version will look like before it is proof printed. This is not to say that the embedded codes have disappeared, and they are still used by some programs. There is often a mode that enables the user to see the raw text plus these codes, and even make changes to the text and the embedded codes.

However, with a modern WYSIWYG desktop publishing program there is no need to use direct coding or even know anything about the method of coding used. You can simply format pages using the palettes, pop-down menus, etc. The program displays a good facsimile of the final printed version, generates the embedded codes, and eventually converts the text and code into the finished product.

Originally it was necessary to understand HTML before you could produce web pages, because there was no WYSIWYG program that would do the job for you. The situation has changed over the years of course, and there are now plenty of programs that enable web pages to be produced by those having no understanding of HTML. In some cases the program may totally shield the user from the underlying HTML code, but even though you can not see it the code is still there. HTML is the language understood by web browsers, and it is what all web site and web page creation programs have to generate.

Roundtrip HTML

Ideally it would be possible to use a WYSIWYG program to generate pages, and then modify the HTML code manually to add special features, sort out minor problems, or whatever. Having made modifications manually, it would still be possible to load the pages into the WYSIWYG HTML editor to make updates. This is called "roundtrip HTML", but it is a feature of few programs. Dreamweaver is a notable exception, and its roundtrip capability has made it the standard choice for professional web site designers.

With most HTML editors that have a WYSIWYG mode you can not manually change the code that is generated. All changes have to be made via the program's tools and menus rather than by direct changes to the HTML. This may seem a rather strange way to do things, but these programs can only handle HTML code written in a specific fashion. Any code produced manually may not conform to the program's way of doing things and can not be interpreted properly. Consequently, you normally have the choice of manually coding pages or using a WYSIWYG HTML program, but not a combination of the two.

For beginners it is probably best to settle for the WYSIWYG option. With this type of program you do not need to know anything about HTML in order to produce web pages. This is not to say that knowledge of HTML brings no advantages. As with many things in computing, the greater your knowledge of how things work, the better the results you are likely to produce. Also, with a deep understanding of how things work you are in a much better position to sort out problems when things do not go according to plan. However, most modern WYSIWYG HTML programs are pretty reliable and sophisticated, rendering knowledge of HTML of relatively little importance if you use this method of page construction.

If you only wish to produce some relatively straightforward web sites there is probably no need to bother too much about learning HTML code, now or ever. If you wish to produce web sites that push the technology to its limits you will certainly have to learn about HTML, and a few other things as well. Even if you decide not to learn HTML coding, I would certainly recommend learning a few basics of this subject, and you will definitely need to understand some of the terminology.

Mark-up

HTML is derived from SGML (standard general mark-up language), which is a standard for the representation of text in digital form. Like Adobe's popular PDF (portable document format) it was designed not to be specific to one type of computer or operating system. This cross platform capability is retained in HTML, and web pages can therefore be viewed correctly on a Mac, a PC using practically any version of Windows, Linux, or whatever, or on any system that has a suitable browser program.

Another reason for the success of HTML is its hyperlink feature, or just plain "links" as they are often called. If you use the Internet you can hardly fail to have met these. Practically every web page has links to other pages in the same site, to pages in other sites, or in some cases to other places on the same over-length web page. Most browsing is done by clicking on links rather than typing web addresses into the browser. It is links that make it possible to surf the Internet.

HTML basics

You can get an example of basic HTML by producing a simple web page using a WYSIWYG page creation program and then looking at the code using a text editor. Some web page creation programs let you see the HTML code that they produce, and Dreamweaver is an example of such a program. A fully working 30-day demonstration version can be downloaded from the www.macromedia.com web site, should you wish

Fig.1.4 Even an empty page has a basic page description

to experiment with this program yourself. To view the HTML code, open the program and then launch the Code Inspector.

Although the default web page will be empty initially, it still has a basic HTML description, and this will be visible in the Code inspector (Figure 1.4). Each HTML page must have certain tags, and these are the HTML, head, title, and body tags. A tag indicates what the code is describing, and in the case of the HTML tag it is the page itself. Many (but not all) tags use opening and closing containers. If you look at the code for the default page you will notice that it starts with "<html>" and finishes with "</html>". These are respectively the opening and closing containers, and because the HTML tag is for the entire page, they appear at the beginning and end of the code.

Most elements of HTML code are comprised of three sections, which are the tag itself, the attribute, and the value. For example, there is a typically a section something like this:

<body bgcolor="#FFFFFF" text="#000000">

</body>

Here body is clearly the tag, and the attribute is "bgcolor", which is the background colour. The attribute is in double quotation marks, and is a numeric value that determines the background colour. Although #FFFFFF may not look like a number, that it is because it is in hexadecimal and not ordinary decimal numbering. Hexadecimal, or just "hex" as it is often called, operates in base 16 and uses numbers from 0 to 9 plus letters from A to F. The hash (#) sign indicates that the number is in hexadecimal and not in decimal. A value of #FFFFFF is the maximum

*Fig.1.5 The highlighted text in the Code Inspector window is the
          HTML code for the picture of an old anchor*

value that can be used and gives a white background. Adding some
text in the Design window, selecting it, and then changing its colour using
the Properties window will result in some code appearing in the Code
window. This will be complete with a six-digit value for the colour.

Dreamweaver lets you alter the code in the code window. If you
experiment with Dreamweaver, try changing the colour value to #AAAAAA
in the Code window and then left-click on the main document window.
This should change the background to a mid-grey colour. Repeat the
process using values of #00FFFF, #FF00FF, and #FFFF00. These should
produce background colours of cyan, magenta, and yellow respectively,
which are the three primary colours. Each primary colour has its own
two-digit strength value, and by using the appropriate value for each
one it is possible to produce any colour within the video system's
repertoire.

Tags

When just about anything is added to an HTML page, at the code level it is a tag plus an attribute and a value. In Figure 1.5 a bitmap image has been added to the page. The image is selected in the design view, so its code is shown highlighted in the Code Inspector to the right of the image. The tag is "<img", and the attribute that follows this is "src", or the source of the image in other words. The value is the path and filename for the image file. It will be apparent from this that the value in HTML code does not have to be a numeric value. It can be whatever data is needed to permit the object to be displayed correctly.

You can learn quite a lot about HTML code simply by adding objects into the design view and then examining the code that Dreamweaver generates. Unlike some WYSIWYG web programs, Dreamweaver produces what is usually efficient and straightforward HTML code, so it is relatively easy to see what is going on. With many programs something as basic as a line of text on an otherwise blank page produces dozens of lines of code. Examining this type of code is likely to make you more confused rather than improve your knowledge of HTML. With Dreamweaver it is usually much easier to see what is going on, and experimenting with it for a while can be quite informative.

Why use HTML?

Using HTML may seem to be doing things the hard way, but there are good reasons for using a mark-up language for web pages. It is possible that we will all have high-speed Internet access before too long, but until then the average Internet connection can only handle data at a rate of a few kilobytes per second. The screen image on an average computer is a bitmap that contains around one to eight megabytes of data. A simple web page sent as a bitmap would require the transfer of a similar amount of data, and a large scrollable page would require a much larger transfer. Data compression techniques could reduce the amounts of data involved, but it could still require something like 100 to 500 kilobytes per page. This represents a download time of around 20 seconds to one minute per page with a 56k modem and a pretty good telephone connection. With a poor connection these times would have to be doubled or trebled, and large pages would extend the download times still further.

Using a mark-up language such as HTML it is possible to reduce simple web pages to just a few kilobytes of data. Complex pages can still require the transfer of substantial amounts of data, especially where large colour photographs are involved. However, HTML helps to keep amounts of data to low levels where this is possible, and keeps download times relatively short. A few compromises may be involved in using a mark-up language, but at present the advantages far outweigh the drawbacks. Where some degree of interactivity is required, simply downloading pages as bitmaps will not give the desired result anyway. With an increasingly interactive Internet there is no real alternative to HTML.

File types

A web page is not usually comprised purely of HTML code with some embedded text. In most cases there will be additional files that the HTML code points to, and the browser then uses these files to complete each page. The most obvious example is a photographic image. The HTML code does not include data for the image, but instead tells the browser which image file to use, its size and position on the page, and anything else needed to get the image displayed correctly on the page. Before creating a web page you will need to have any additional files present on your PC and in a suitable file format. These are the most important of the standard file types used with web pages:

Jpeg or Jpg

Whether called Jpeg or Jpg, it is pronounced jay-peg. This is now the most common format used for bit maps. A bitmap is an image that is made up of dots, or pixels as they are termed. A computer monitor produces images in this fashion, and any type of graphic can be represented as a bitmap. However, it produces large files and often gives relatively poor results when applied to line drawings. This file format is mainly used with photographic images, or pseudo photographic images, where it enables good results to be obtained without resorting to large file sizes. The modest file size is achieved using compression, and with some graphics programs you can use varying degrees of compression and up to three different types.

Note that the small file sizes obtained when using high degrees of compression are obtained at the expense of reduced picture quality. In Internet applications it is clearly helpful to have small files in order to keep download times to a minimum. On the other hand, there is no point in having an image that downloads quickly if no one can see what it is meant to be! The borderline between acceptable and unacceptable quality is a subjective matter, and can only be determined using the "suck it and see" approach.

GIF

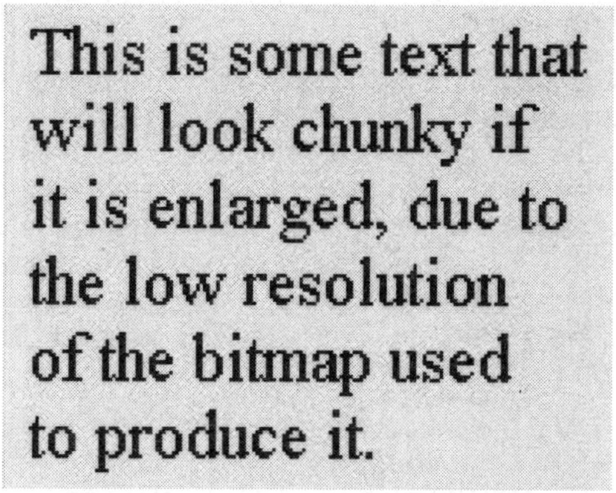

The full name for this format is CompuServe GIF, and programs that use it have to be licensed by CompuServe. This format is generally preferred for line art such as graphs and most diagrams, or practically any non-photographic images. In fact the GIF image format is sometimes used for

Fig.1.6 *Bitmaps tend to give poor results when enlarged*

monochrome photographs, but these days Jpeg is the more popular choice for images of this type. With suitable images it combines small file sizes and high quality. Up to 256 colours are- supported, and these can be any colours rather than those from a predetermined set. No compression is used with this format, but the file sizes are kept small by the inherently compact method of storing images.

With a line art format the image is stored on the basis of (say) a line of a certain width going from one co-ordinate to another, rather than as a set of pixels to depict the line. An advantage of this system is that images are produced in high quality on high-resolution printers, etc. The higher the resolution of the output device, the higher the quality of reproduction with line art images. Bitmap images, unless very large numbers of pixels are used, produce rather chunky looking results when printed large. Figure 1.6 shows an example of this effect. GIF files can be used for simple animations incidentally.

Png

This is a relatively new image file format, and it is apparently pronounced pong, as in nasty smell or Ping-Pong. It is designed to be a sort of universal licence-free image format that will eventually replace the GIF format. Although relatively new, any reasonably modern browser should be able to handle Png images (Internet Explorer 4 or later for example). These days many image editing programs can export images in this format, but it is probably better to save photographic images as Jpeg files.

Txt

This is a simple text file, and any word processor or text editor should be able to produce a file in this format. It is important to realise that this type of file can only handle basic text, and that all or virtually all formatting information is lost when a file is saved in this format. Hard carriage returns should be retained, but text size, font, and colour information are lost. Tabulation tends to go astray when text is swapped using this format. You can include txt files in your web sites, and any browser should display them properly, but due to their limitations txt files are not often used in this way.

The normal way of using a txt file is to use a word processor to generate blocks of text which are then imported into a web page creation program. Any formatting is then applied using that program. This is not necessarily the best way of doing things though. Using the ordinary Copy and Paste facilities to transfer text from a word processor to the page creation program might retain some formatting information. This is by no means certain, but it is worth trying it to see. It might be better to export the text in HTML format. In practice this method will not always give perfect results every time, but no more than a small amount of editing should be needed to restore any lost formatting. Most modern word processors such as Microsoft's Word can save documents in HTML format.

Other formats

There are other file formats in use on the Internet, but most of these are not used in quite the same way as (say) a Jpeg image that forms part of a web page when it is viewed using a browser. It is more usual for these other file formats to be downloaded and then viewed and (or) heard via a suitable program such as a media player. Many of these files can be handled by the Microsoft Media Player, but some require a player specifically designed for that type of file. Some of the more common of these media file types are listed here:

Aif or Aiff

A sound file format. File types are usually indicated by a three or four letter extension to the filename. For instance, a file called myphoto1.jpg would be a bitmap image in Jpeg format. Three letter extensions were used in the days of MS/DOS, but this limit is not present in modern operating systems. However, some people still use three letter extensions, and it is for this reason that some extensions exist in three and four letter versions. Thus, a Jpeg image file can have jpg or jpeg as its extension, and this audio format can have Aif or Aiff as the extension.

AVI

A movie format that can also handle sound. Some AVI files require additional decoding, and will only play if the appropriate decoder is installed. The additional software is commonly called a codec (encoder/decoder), but only the decoder part is needed for playback. DivX is by far the most common add-on codec for AVI files. AVI files can be played using the Windows Media Player, as can DivX encoded files provided the appropriate codec is installed.

Mpeg or Mpg

Another movie format that can handle sound as well and the nearest thing to a standard movie format for Internet use. The Windows Media Player can be used to playback Mpeg files.

Mov

Apple QuickTime movie/animation files. The Apple Quicktime player is needed in order to play back these files.

Swf

Files in Macromedia Flash format. These are used to provide animations including fancy rollovers, etc. A player program is needed to play flash files, but these days the player is sometimes installed as standard with the browser.

PDF

This is the Adobe portable document format. It is actually a general-purpose file format that can handle text and any type of image. This book was sent to the printers in the form of a PDF file for example. A high degree of compression is used, but results of excellent quality are produced. Adobe Acrobat reader is needed to view PDF files, but the reader program is free from the Adobe web site and is available for several types of computer and various operating systems. The popular web browsers link to the reader program so that they can effectively be used to display PDF documents. This format is a popular choice for complex and (or) large documents.

MP3

An audio format that uses a large amount of compression but still manages to produce some impressive results. This is probably the nearest thing to a standard audio file format.

WMA and WMV

These are Windows media files, and are respectively for audio and video files. Of course, the video version can include sound as well. They have been somewhat overshadowed by the MP3, AVI, and MPG file formats, but are nevertheless in widespread use.

MIDI

MIDI was originally designed for use with synthesisers and other electronic musical instruments. A MIDI file can be played by having a synthesiser connected to the MIDI port of a computer, but these days most sound cards can play MIDI files, albeit with a fair amount of help from the soundcard's driver software.

DHTML

DHTML is an extension of HTML that uses a variety of technologies to permit clever things to be achieved. For example, graphics or other objects can change when the pointer is placed over them, or other things can change when the pointer is at a certain point on the page. These are languages that DHTML uses in addition to standard HTML, with a brief explanation of each one.

JavaScript

This should not be confused with the Java programming language, which is completely different. The Java name was licensed by Netscape from Sun Microsystems, but only the name was used, not Java technology. JavaScript is now very popular and is used to add all manner of clever tricks to web sites. It is often used to provide better interactivity with the user. For instance, many financial web sites can produce graphs showing price data for shares and this type of thing. Without JavaScript a chart has no interactive capability. If you wish to zoom in on part of the chart, either it is not possible at all, or fresh parameters have to be set and then the chart is redrawn "from scratch". With JavaScript charts you can use the mouse to indicate the part of the chart that is of interest, and then you get a zoomed view of that section.

Using JavaScript it is rather like using a charting application on your computer rather than just downloading web pages, and I suppose that when using JavaScript you are downloading and using a program on your computer. JavaScript is used in other ways, such as for rollovers and testing browser compatibility. Note that you do not have to learn JavaScript in order to use it. Like HTML, there are now programs such as Dreamweaver that will automatically generate simple JavaScript programs. If you should decide to learn JavaScript it is more difficult to master than HTML, but should not be difficult for anyone having some previous programming experience.

CSS

CSS stands for Cascading Style Sheets. This is a relatively new page layout system but it is supported by any reasonably up to date browser. It is designed to give better and more precise control over page layouts than HTML.

DOM

DOM is the acronym for document object module, and it provides a link to external scripting and programming protocols such as ActiveX. It also enables so-called plug-ins to be used, such as Flash or Shockwave.

XML

XML (Extensible Mark-up Language), like HTML, is based on SGML. Extensible simply means that it can be extended, and it is extended by designers creating their own tags. XML is a subject that goes beyond the scope of this book.

Page elements

We now have the basic elements for a web page. The HTML code describes the page, telling the browser what to put where. Text will usually be within the HTML code, but any graphics, sound or movie files will be stored in separate files. The HTML code then points to these so that the browser can find them. In the case of image files the code will give page position and size information so that the image is displayed correctly. The HTML code includes similar information for the text so that it is displayed in the correct font, etc., and there is further code to describe the basic parameters of the page itself (title information, background colour, and so on).

Modern WYSIWYG web page creation programs do a good job of hiding HTML and its limitations from the user, but you do not really have quite the degree of freedom available with a desktop publishing program. The original version of HTML was somewhat limited in scope, and it is for this reason that HTML has been continuously expanded and equipped with ever more add-ons. Unless you are going to produce nothing more than a few very basic web pages it is helpful to understand the limitations and some of the methods used to extend HTML's capabilities.

CGI, etc.

When you go in search of a web host for your site you will find that most of these companies have free Perl and CGI (common gateway interface) scripts, FrontPage extensions, and the like. A degree of interactivity with users is possible using JavaScript and some of the other facilities described so far, but the possibilities are relatively limited. With some types of site it is necessary for information to be taken from users and stored on the server so that it can be viewed by other users, or perhaps so that it can be used by the owner of the site. A bulletin board is a common example of users needing to input information so that other users can view it.

This type of thing is usually handled by a program running on the server, and this is where Perl, CGI, and the like come into play. If you wish to use any facility of this type it is important to make sure that your web host has facilities to support it. Support of this type will usually be available if you are paying for the web hosting. In fact the web space provider may well have free scripts or programs that you can use. Note that it is unlikely that any support of this type will be available if you are using web space provided free by your Internet service provider (ISP), or if you are using any other type of free web hosting.

Initially it is probably best not to bother too much about advanced features such as drop-down menus and complex interactivity. This would be a case of "learning to walk before you can crawl", and initially it is better to opt for a relatively simple site that works well rather than a complex one that could be of dubious reliability, if you ever manage to finish it. Programs that are not implemented properly can crash a server and all the sites running on it. You therefore need to know exactly what you are doing with this type of thing, as you could otherwise find your web hosting contract cancelled.

Entering text

With desktop publishing programs and word processors a carriage return is normally used to indicate a new line, and two carriage returns are used to start a new paragraph. In HTML tags are used to indicate line and paragraph breaks. These tags are <br> for a line break, <p> to start a paragraph,

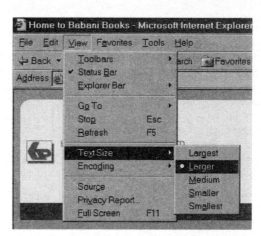

Fig.1.7 Internet Explorer offers five text sizes

and </p> to end a paragraph. A space approximately equal to two lines is placed between paragraphs. The page creation program you use might convert carriage returns into the appropriate tags, but it is often necessary to insert line and paragraph breaks using a toolbar or menu.

In a similar vein, you might find that pressing the spacebar once has the desired effect, but operating it two or more times in succession still only adds one space. Further spaces can be added using the non-breaking space character, which should be available from a toolbar or menu.

Windows programs normally permit text sizes from about 5 to 72 points to be used, but a much more limited range of sizes is available using basic HTML. The system used in HTML is to have a base font size, with other sizes being set relative to this. The actual base size is determined by the browser used to display the page, and there is usually an option to make the text larger or smaller. Internet Explorer 6 for example, has the option of two larger and two smaller settings (Figure 1.7). At the normal setting, the base size is usually around 10 to 14 points.

The example text shown in Figure 1.8 was produced using Netobjects Fusion, and this provides the usual seven sizes. These are comprised of the base size (size 0), plus two smaller and four larger sizes. The character at the end of all but the bottom line indicates that Fusion has inserted a paragraph tag. It automatically adds a paragraph tag when a carriage

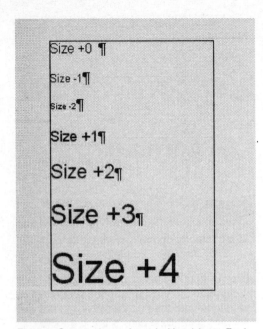

Fig.1.8 Seven sizes of text in Netobjects Fusion

return is used or a line break if a soft return (Shift – Return) is used. Of course, the tag symbols do not appear when the page is viewed using a browser. Fusion, like most web page creation programs, provides the option of switching them off so that the text can be viewed as it will appear in a browser.

Headings

Headings and subheadings are useful for breaking up large chunks of text and for generally improving the appearance of pages. It is possible to use the larger text sizes for headings, but HTML has special facilities for headings. The main one is the heading tag (<h#>), where the number in the tag selects one of six predefined heading text styles. By default, the heading styles are usually in bold text of various sizes. Figure 1.9 shows the default heading styles of Fusion. The numbering system operates in the opposite manner to the one you would probably expect, with the highest number giving the smallest text size. The heading styles can be redefined, and in Figure 1.10 the h6 tag has been redefined to produce a larger text size in a different font.

The normal text formatting tools are available. The text and background colours can be changed, centre, left, and right alignments are available, and some programs also offer full justification. Various fonts are available, but you have to bear in mind that the fonts available on your PC will not necessarily be available on the PCs used to access your web site. Using the more common fonts runs little risk of things going seriously awry, but using some of the more zany fonts could result in user's browsers substituting an unsuitable font.

Where a heading in a large and unusual font is required, the safest method is to use a graphics program to produce the headline and then save it as an image file. This image file is used on the web page in the normal way. The drawback of this method is that it gives relatively long download times, although it is unlikely to make a vast difference. For most web use a simple font is better than a serif type (one with curly bits). When displayed on a monitor, plain fonts such as Arial, Helvetica, and Swiss 721 are generally easier to read than serif fonts such as the ever popular Times New Roman.

Text colours, background colours, text alignment, and so on, are all handled in HTML by the relevant tags. However, with a WYSIWYG web page creation program you simply select the required parameters using the usual toolbars, dialogue

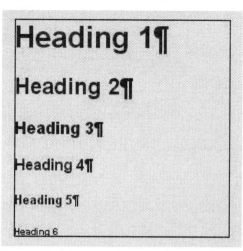

Fig.1.9 The six default heading styles in Fusion

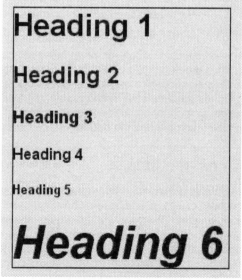

Fig.1.10 The h6 tag has been redefined to produce a larger text size in a different font

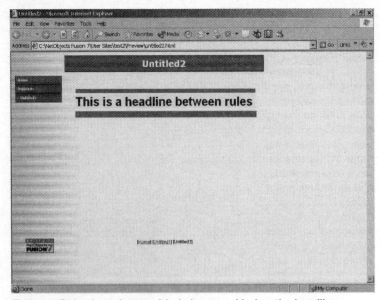

Fig.1.11 Rules have been added above and below the headline

boxes, menus, or whatever. Most of the text handling is similar to using a word processor or a desktop publishing program to format text, but with what is usually a few less options available. The web page creation program generates the appropriate HTML code for the formatting you select, complete with all the necessary tags. With luck, it then displays properly using any of the popular web browsers.

Lines and lists

Horizontal lines, or rules as they are also known, are useful for separating sections of a page, emphasising headlines, and generally making a page look prettier. They can be used quite effectively in conjunction with variations in the background colour. Any page creation program should enable rules to be dragged to the required length and give control of the line width. There might be other facilities, to enable the line to be hollow or filled for example. Figure 1.11 shows a dummy page produced using Netobjects Fusion, and this has rules of different thicknesses above and below a headline.

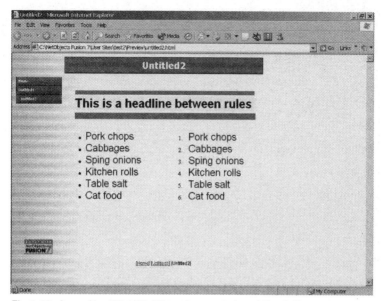

Fig.1.12 An ordered list (right) and an unordered list (left)

Bulleted and numbered lists can be produced using HTML, but in HTML terminology they are respectively called unordered and ordered lists. With a WYSIWYG page creation program it is normally very easy to produce lists. Each item in the list is added using the normal text facilities, with each item on a separate line. Do not use soft carriage returns to separate entries as you will probably find that everything in the list is considered to be the first and only entry. Only use soft returns to spread a single entry over more than one line. Figure 1.12 shows the dummy page with an ordered list and an unordered type added.

Tables

Tables were originally introduced into HTML as a means of displaying things like scientific and financial data in tabular form. However, the use of HTML tables has expanded beyond basic functions such as these, and tables can be used for aligning images and other tasks. In fact tables be used to control the layout of entire pages, and often are used in this fashion. Therefore, even though tables may seem to be irrelevant to the types of web site you will be producing, it is as well to learn

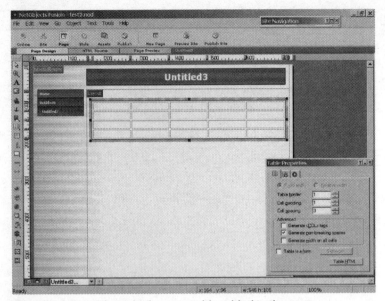

Fig.1.13 A five column by four row table added to the page

something about them. They can be extremely useful if used in the right way, and you will probably use them a great deal.

When generating a table you have to specify the number of rows and columns required. Figure 1.13 shows a table having five columns by four rows that has been added to a page under construction in Fusion. In this initial form a table is not particularly useful apart from use with tables of data. However, the cell walls can be dragged to new positions, and the cells do not have to be of uniform size (Figure 1.14). The basic column and row structure must be retained when using the dragging method, but the column widths and row heights are all adjustable.

The versatility of tables goes beyond this, since it is possible to split and merge cells. This enables a table to break away from a rigid row and cell structure with all cells in the same row having the same height, and all cells in the same column having the same width. In Figure 1.15 one cell has been made much larger than the others and a background image has been added to it. Although it has been added as a background, there is no intention in this case of adding anything on top of it. This has just been used as a means of adding an image to the cell. Above this a

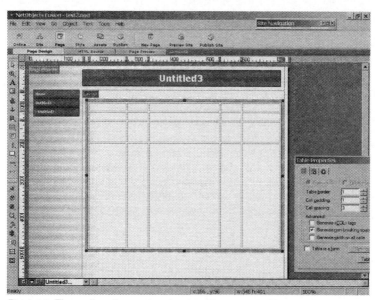

Fig.1.14 The cell walls can be dragged to new positions

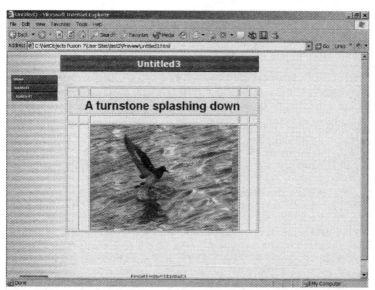

Fig.1.15 Five cells have been merged into one to take the headline

row of cells has been merged into one very wide cell. The background colour was then changed, and a centre aligned heading was added.

This gives an indication of what can be achieved using tables, but with a little time and effort it is possible to accommodate practically any page layout using tables. With many programs you have the option of converting a conventional HTML layout into a table based type. This will often give more precise results when the page is displayed using a browser. The conversion can also be used to tidy up slightly wonky page layouts. Remember that a table does not have to be used to control the layout of an entire page. A table can cover as little or as much of a page as you require it to. Some programs enable tables to be nested. In other words, a table can be inserted into a cell of an existing table. I suppose that using tables within tables is potentially useful, but it is probably best not to get carried away with this type of thing.

Padding and spacing

When using tables you will certainly encounter the terms "padding" and "spacing". The padding parameter of a cell enables its contents to be kept away from the cell outline. In other words, a margin of the specified width is inserted around the contents but within the confines of the cell. It is advisable to use at least a small amount of padding with text, which can otherwise be difficult to read as it tends to merge with the cell walls. The spacing parameter controls the amount of space between the pairs of lines used for the cell walls.

The width of a table can be specified as a certain number of pixels or as a percentage. If it is specified in pixels, then it will always be displayed at that size in the browser. With a large table this might mean that some users have to scroll around the page in order to see all the contents. Where the width is specified as a percentage, its size in pixels will depend on the size of the browser's window. This avoids the need for scrolling, but the contents of the table might be reformatted to suit different table sizes in pixels. This will not necessarily matter, but it could make a mess of your carefully designed layouts.

Frames

Frames are a feature of many web sites these days and they seem to be found on most commercial sites. Using frames a web page can be divided into sections, with each one containing a separate HTML document. In other words, you effectively have HTML pages within an

HTML page. A common use of this feature is to have (say) the left-hand section of the screen devoted to a list of contents complete with links, and perhaps including a brief summary of each page. This is often referred to as the "navigation" frame. The centre and right-hand section of the screen is devoted to an introductory document giving details of the company, organisation, or whatever. Frames can have independent scrollbars, so the navigation frame can be fixed while the introductory document can be scrollable. This keeps the entire navigation frame instantly accessible at all times, since scrolling down the main document leaves the navigation links in position.

In fact many sites have this arrangement for every page in the site, so that users always have easy access to every part of the site. The larger frames are often called the "content" frames, because they have the actual content of the site. With frames it is easy to produce sites based on this arrangement, with one HTML page (the navigation page) always visible. Links in the navigation frame can load new documents into the content frame. If you have something like 30 pages in the site, you only have to make an initial page having the two frames, plus 29 ordinary HTML documents. The 49 ordinary documents are loaded into the content frame, as and when necessary, via links in the navigation frame. This avoids having to make 30 pages with the navigation section included on every one of them.

Of course, with frames you are not limited to this basic two-page arrangement, and it is possible to have numerous frames per page. However, the more complicated the arrangement the greater the opportunity for things to go wrong, so it is best to settle for relatively simple arrangements at first. Most sites can actually be accommodated perfectly well by a simple twin-frame arrangement of the type outlined previously.

It is only fair to point out that frames are not universally popular, and there are plenty of good sites that are totally frame-free. One advantage of frames is that they are popular with users, since they can make site navigation much simpler. Frames also make it easier to update a site. There is just one navigation frame to update rather than having to alter what could otherwise be dozens of pages. On the downside, frames can be confusing if the site is not well designed, and many feel that frame based sites are aesthetically challenged.

There can also be practical problems with frame based sites. For instance, in order to print out an entire page it is normally necessary to print the frames one by one, although some printer drivers include the options of printing the current frame or all of them. Like any facility of

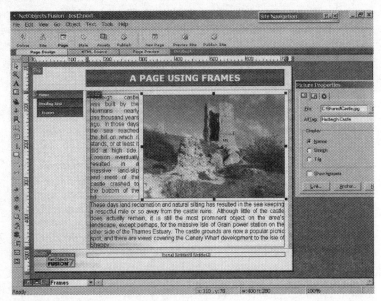

Fig.1.16 A page produced using one of Fusion's predefined framesets

any program, frames should not be used simply because they are there. However, it is certainly worth learning the basics of frames and using them where appropriate. They are probably not appropriate when building relatively simple sites.

Framesets

In order to fully understand the use of frames you have to understand framesets. In the example arrangement described previously there are three documents involved. The navigation and content documents constitute two of these, and the third is the page that contains the two frames into which the other two documents are fitted. This third document that contains the other two is the frameset. A web page creation program that can handle frames will usually have several predefined framesets that make it easy to produce standard layouts. With the more upmarket programs you can define your own, and you have to get more deeply involved with framesets. Fortunately, for most purposes the predefined framesets will suffice.

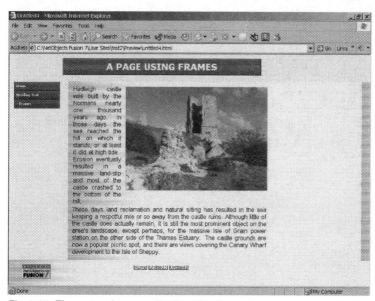

Fig.1.17 The example page displayed using a browser

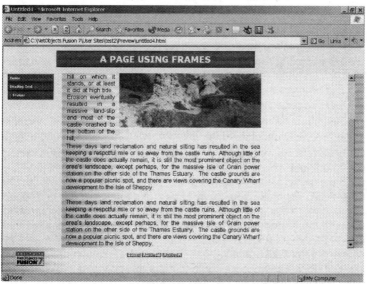

Fig.1.18 Scrolling the content frame does not alter the navigation frame

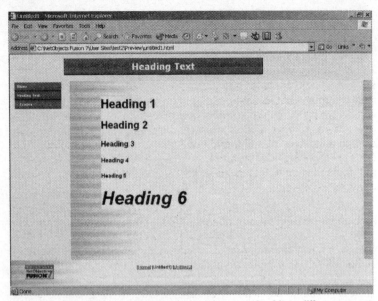

Fig.1.19   Operating a navigation button has resulted in a different page being displayed in the content frame

Figure 1.16 shows a dummy web page produced using Fusion and one of its predefined framesets. The left-hand frame is used for navigation, the one at the top contains a heading, and the right-hand frame is used for the main subject matter. There is a fourth frame at the bottom, but this has no proper content and has simply been left in its default state. In a real web page this would probably be used for something like contact information. Figure 1.17 shows the dummy page displayed using a browser, and the original layout has been faithfully retained.

In Figure 1.18 the main content frame has been enlarged by duplicating the lower block of text. This makes it too large to be displayed in full by the browser, so a vertical scrollbar has been added. There will usually be a facility to make scrollbars appear automatically, as and when necessary and this will usually be the default option. Note how scrolling down to the bottom of the main content frame has only scrolled that frame. All the other frames remain completely unchanged. Figure 1.19 shows the result of operating one of the navigation buttons. This has brought up the appropriate content in the main content frame, but the other frames have again been left unaltered.

Adding links

It may be "love that makes the world go round", but it is that other four letter word beginning with "l" that makes the Internet go round. While using the Internet you click on one link after another. Links enable users to move around web sites with just a few clicks of the mouse, and move from site to site just as easily. People can and do surf the net for hours without typing in a single web address. Unless you put in links to enable users to easily move around your web sites they will probably give up and go elsewhere. Links that do not work properly are another "sure fire" way of getting rid of visitors to your site. It is the links from one page of the site to another that make it a web site rather than just a collection of separate pages.

Links to other sites are perhaps less important, and on the face of it there is no point in making it easy for people to leave your site and go elsewhere. However, if everyone took this attitude it would become much more difficult to navigate the Internet and find what you require. The secret of success with links to other sites is reciprocity, or "I'll scratch your back if you scratch mine" if you prefer. Provide links to other relevant web sites, but try to make sure that plenty of other sites have links that bring users to your site as well.

Relative links

Hyperlinks, or just plain "links" as they are often called these days, provide a quick way of directing a browser from one page to another. The page containing the link is the "referring" page, and the one that it is linked to is the "target" page. Obviously the link on the referring page must include the path and filename for the target page so that the browser knows exactly where to go. Web pages can be addressed using absolute or relative addresses. A link to another web site must use absolute addressing, which means that the full web address (URL) must be specified.

Links within a site are usually relative, but relative to what? Internal links normally use addressing that is relative to the site's root directory. With this method the path to the target file is given with the site's root directory acting as the starting point. The root directory is the one that contains the index file that produces the homepage. This method of addressing is essentially the same as the system used for hard disc drives.

Some programs such as Dreamweaver also support document relative path names, which use the subfolder of the referring page as the starting point for the path. This is very convenient when linking to a page in the same subfolder, since no path is needed. To link to a page called "castle.htm" in the same folder as the referring page the target would simply be given as "castle.htm". Giving the path to somewhere lower in the directory structure is also very simple. Suppose that this target file was in a subfolder called "tourism", and that this branched directly from the subfolder containing the referring page. The path and filename for the target would be "\tourism\castle.htm".

Matters are a little more complex if the target is in a subfolder that is higher in the directory structure, or it is in a subfolder that has its origins higher in the directory structure. In either case it is still possible to use a document relative path, and two full stop characters (..) are used to indicate each move up one level in the directory structure. Consider these two paths and filenames:

../castle.htm

../../places/castle.htm

In the first example the file is in the folder one level higher up the directory structure. This is indicated by the two full stops at the beginning of the path. In the second example there are two pairs of full stops, indicating that the file is two levels further up the directory structure. However, it is then down one level in a subfolder called "places". Using this method it is possible to provide a path to anywhere in a local site, from anywhere within that site, but the site-root relative method is the simpler of the two systems. If you use a link that is relative to the referring page, always make sure that the page has been saved first. Until the page is saved there is nothing for the link to be relative to.

Relocating

Of course, the point of using relative links internally is that they will always find the target, even if the site is relocated. Remember that the normal site creation process is to first build a local site, which means a site located on a disc drive in your PC. The completed site is then uploaded to a server where the site is hosted. The important point here is that the location of the site on your hard disc will be different to its location on the disc in the server. Absolute links are therefore likely to miss their targets because they will point to the wrong root folder or perhaps even the wrong disc. A relative link will still work because it operates relative to a folder in the site, which gives a certain starting point. It does not matter where in the folder structure that folder is located, or even which disc it is

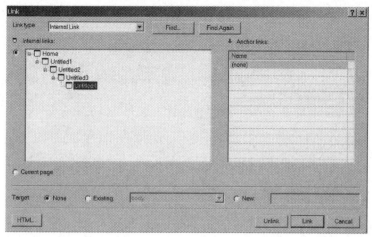

Fig.1.20 The Link window of Fusion

on. Provided the file and folder structure has not been altered, the links will still work.

Most web page creation programs make it easy to add links, and the user does not have to bother too much about the technicalities. Adding a link using Fusion is just a matter of selecting the object to be linked, which in most cases will be a piece of text, and then operating the Link button. This produces a window like the one of Figure 1.20. By default the Internal Link option is selected, and the file and folder structure of the site is shown in the main panel. In order to link to a page it is merely necessary to double-click its entry or select its entry and operate the link button.

When text is used as a link, it will be underlined and changed to the default colour for linked text. This is usually but not always blue, but with most programs a different colour can be used. In Figure 1.21 the line of text at the bottom has been used as a link. Note that you do not have to use complete blocks of text or even complete words as links. As little as one character can be selected and used as a link.

The Link type menu of Fusion has other options, including Files, which could be used to provide a link to a PDF file for example. There is also an External Link option which produces the modified window of Figure 1.22. Adding the link is just a matter of inserting the appropriate web address in the textbox and operating the Link button.

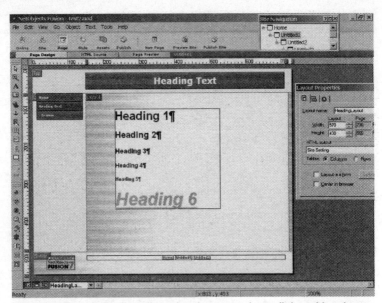

*Fig.1.21 The bottom line of text has been used as a link and has been
set at the default colour for link text*

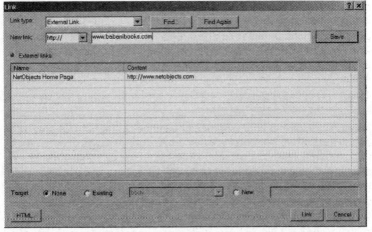

Fig.1.22 The Link window when used to select an external link

Fig.1.23 A four-sided polygon has been drawn around the tower

Hot spots

Images are linked in much the same way as text, but links from images have an interesting optional extra in the form of multiple links. In other words, rather than linking the entire image to one page, separate parts of the image can be linked to different pages. In Fusion there are three versions of the Hotspot button that provide circular, rectangular, and polygonal hotspots. With the circular and rectangular versions it is just a matter of dragging the shape to the required size and position on the image. With the polygonal version it is a matter of placing points on the image to define the outline.

In Figure 1.23 four points have been added using the polygonal version of the Hotspot tool, and these provide an outline that roughly corresponds to the outline of the castle tower. When the page is viewed in a browser, placing the pointer over the tower results in the usual Alt text appearing near the pointer. Additionally, the pointer changes to the hand symbol (Figure 1.24), indicating that the pointer is over a link. Moving the pointer outside the hotspot results in the pointer returning to the standard version, indicating that the rest of the image is not acting as a link (Figure 1.25). A number of links can be added to an image by using further hotspots.

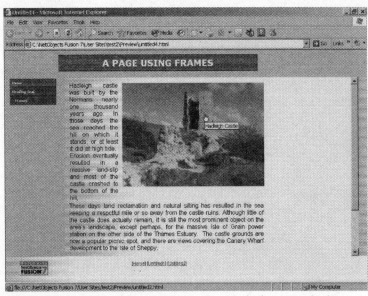

Fig.1.24 The pointer changes to a hand symbol when over the hotspot

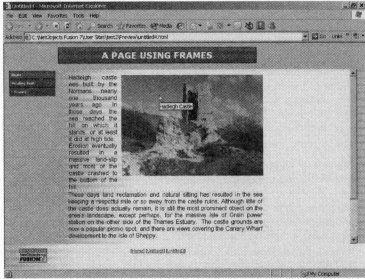

Fig.1.25 The rest of the image does not act as a link

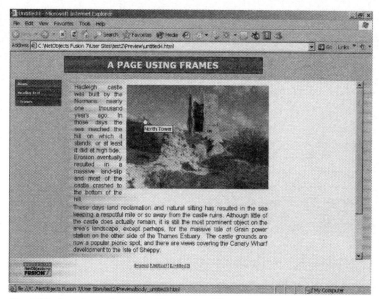

Fig.1.26 A rectangular link with its own Alt text has been added

In Figure 1.26 a rectangular link has been added and it has also been given its own Alt text.

Named anchors

The links covered so far are the most common type where the link takes the user to a new web page. There is another type that takes the user to a particular point on a page, and these are known as "named anchors" or just "anchors". There is obviously little point in using a named anchor on a small page that can be viewed in totality on the average monitor, or which requires minimal scrolling in order to view the whole page. This type of link is used in long pages that have to be viewed bit by bit, with perhaps only about 10 percent of the page being visible at any one time. In general, this type of page is best avoided, and in most cases it is better if very large amounts of material are broken up into separate pages of moderate size.

The long page option tends to be taken where there is not enough material to fully merit breaking things up into several separate pages, but there is too much material to be used easily as a single page. It is also popular

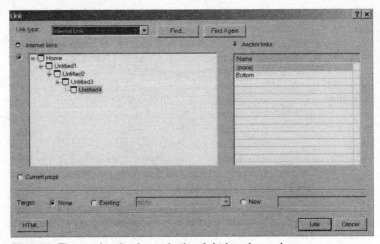

Fig.1.27 The anchor is shown in the right-hand panel

where something like a series of news stories has to be put together and published on the web as quickly as possible. This could be done as separate pages, but one large page is easier to put together and test. A list of contents is used at the top of the page, with each item in the list linking to a named anchor in the relevant part of the page. By left-clicking on an item in the list a user is immediately taken to the relevant part of the page.

Each section of the page normally has a link back to the top of the page, so that it is easy to return to the list to select another section of the document. The single page method is slow initially because there is a large page to download. However, thereafter the system is very quick, and left-clicking on a link produces an almost instant response. This is due to the fact that there is nothing to load when a link is activated. The browser just has to move to a new point in the page that has already downloaded.

With Fusion an anchor is added by placing the text cursor at the appropriate point within some text and then operating the Link button. This produces a small dialogue box where a name for the anchor is added. Linking to an anchor is much the same as linking to a page or file. First the required text, image, or whatever is selected and then the link button is operated. This produces the usual link window, and the name of the anchor should be included in the right-hand section of the

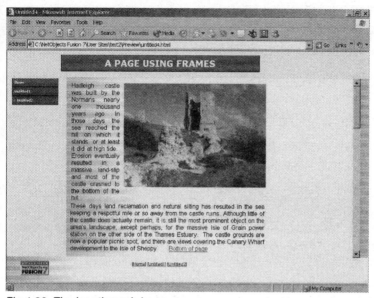

Fig.1.28 The lengthened dummy page

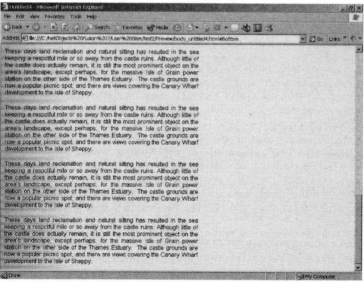

Fig.1.29 Activating the link has scrolled the page down to the anchor

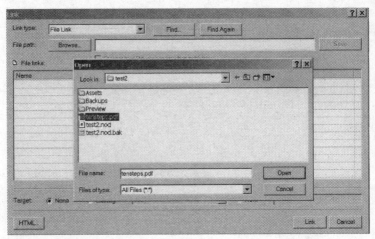

Fig.1.30 A file browser can be used to locate the required file

window. For this example I added more duplicate blocks of text to the page with an anchor called "bottom" at the bottom of the page. This anchor is shown in the right-hand section of the Link window (Figure 1.27), and a link to it is added by double-clicking on its entry.

Figure 1.28 shows the top section of the modified page, with the link text near the bottom of the visible section of the page. Activating this link scrolled to the anchor at the bottom of the page, as can be seen in Figure 1.29. Anchors are often used as a quick means of scrolling to the top or bottom of long pages.

Linking files

Most links are to web pages, but sometimes links to files are used. Adding a link to a file is usually handled in much the same way as a link to a web page. In Fusion there is a specific option for files (Figure 1.30). The filename with full path can be entered in the textbox, but the easier and more reliable method is to operate the Browse button and use the file browser.

The result of operating a link to a file is usually rather different to operating a link to an ordinary HTML web page. Precisely what happens when linking to a file depends on the type of file concerned. In the case of an ordinary text file it should be displayed by the browser, but there is no

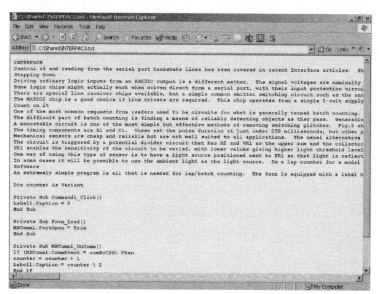

Fig.1.31 Text files can be displayed by a browser

Fig.1.32 A PDF file being displayed within Internet Explorer

1   Basic elements

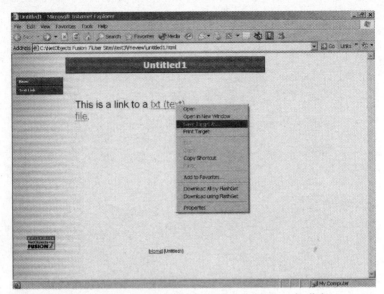

Fig.1.33 A file can be downloaded by right-clicking on its link

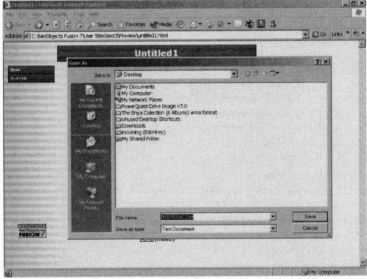

Fig.1.34 The usual Save As window appears when downloading a file

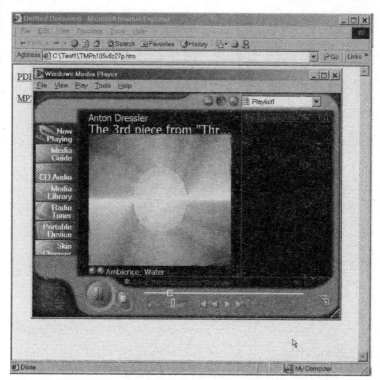

Fig.1.35 The Windows Media Player has been launched to play an MP3 file

significant formatting with this type of file, and you can sometimes find that the lines of text are very long (Figure 1.31). A PDF file is often used when it is necessary to have long and (or) complicated documents on a web site. This requires the free Adobe Acrobat Reader program, and this will run from within Internet Explorer (Figure 1.32).

With some types of file the browser will assume that you wish to download the file. This will usually happen with program (exe) files and archive files such as zip and rar types. Any file can be downloaded by right-clicking on the link and selecting Save Target As from the popup menu (Figure 1.33). This produces the usual file browser so that the file can be saved in the required location (Figure 1.34). The file name can be changed if required. This is a standard facility of web browsers, but it is a good idea to provide brief instructions on downloading a file in appropriate cases.

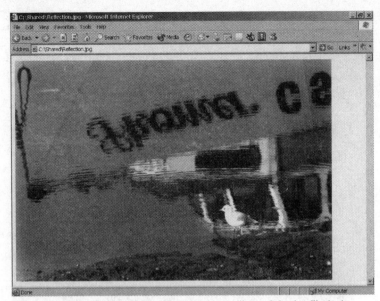

Fig.1.36 Activating a link to a Jpeg image will result in the file being displayed by the browser

Multimedia

Multimedia files such as Mpeg movies and MP3 audio files require a player program. Some can be played with the Windows Media Player, but others require a special player program. Provided a suitable player program, etc., is installed, operating a link to a multimedia file should result in the player being launched and the file being played (Figure 1.35). It is a good idea to include at least a brief explanation of what is required to play or display any file that requires something more than a normal browser. Also provide details if an additional codec is needed. Ideally you should include the web address where a suitable player, codec, or whatever can be downloaded.

Note that image files, provided they are in a normal Internet file format such as Jpeg, will be displayed properly in a browser. Figure 1.36 shows a Jpeg image being displayed in a browser, but the image is not in an HTML page. The Jpeg file was directly accessed using a link. Using a file format that is not a standard type for web use will result in an image file being treated like any other "mystery" file, and it will be assumed that

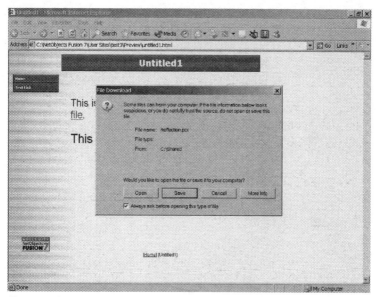

*Fig.1.37 Activating a link to an image in a non-web format image
results in the options of opening or saving it*

the user wishes to download it. In Figure 1.37 the Jpeg file has been
replaced with one for the same image but in PCX format. Operating the
link has resulted in the File Download window duly appearing. There is
also the option of opening the file, but this is only possible if the PC is
equipped with a program that can handle the appropriate file type.

Software

It is possible to produce web sites without buying any software, but the
totally free approach does limit your options. One way of producing a
web site is to go to a web publishing site where a site can be built using
the facilities available at that site. This type of site construction has
become more sophisticated over the years, and it is actually possible to
produce good quality sites using this approach. Unless you are prepared
to settle for a text-only site, or one illustrated with clipart, an image editing
program will be needed in order to prepare images for web use. The
subjects of web publishing and dealing with web images are covered in
chapters three and four respectively.

1 Basic elements

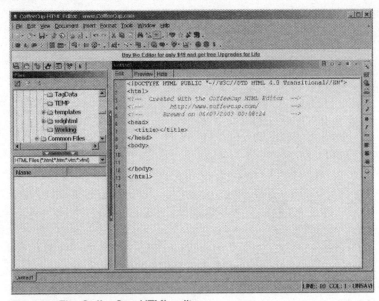

Fig.1.38 The CoffeeCup HTML editor

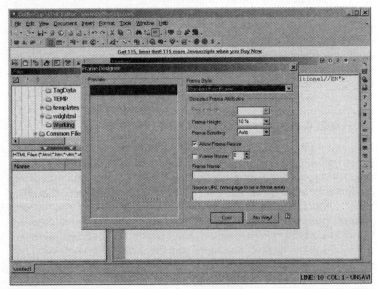

Fig.1.39 Code can be generated automatically

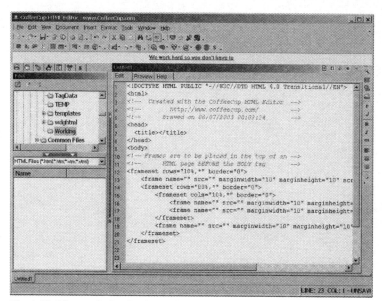

Fig.1.40   The code for the frame has been added in the right-hand window

HTML is just text, so it is possible to produce web pages using a text editor or word processor if you have a suitably deep knowledge of HTML coding. Something as basic as the Windows Notepad text editor can be used to produce web pages using this method. Even if your knowledge of HTML is adequate, this is not a quick or easy way of doing things. The code has to be checked using a browser, and it can take a lot of "fine tuning" to get everything just right.

There are HTML editors that are mostly free or quite inexpensive. A modern HTML editor can provide a fair amount of help with the HTML coding, but you still need to have a good knowledge of HTML in order to produce web pages this way. Figure 1.38 shows the CoffeeCup HTML editor in operation. The code in the right-hand section of the screen provides the basis for the page, and is provided by the program. Additional code can be entered manually or generated automatically. In Figure 1.39 the Frame button has been operated and the Frame Designer dialogue box has appeared. The required parameters are selected and the corresponding HTML code is then generated automatically (Figure 1.40).

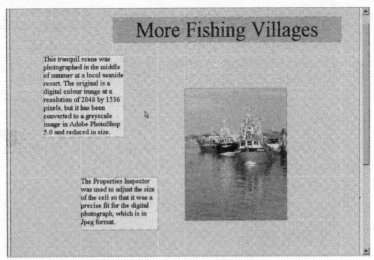

Fig.1.41   The layout as it appears in Dreamweaver

WYSIWYG

Using a good HTML editor is quicker and easier than writing all the code from scratch, but it is still quite time consuming to check pages and make the corrections necessary to make them display exactly as required. What you see is what you get (WYSIWYG) web page creation programs take things a stage further and enable the pages to be produced in much the same way as using a desktop publishing program. Text is placed on the page and moved, formatted, and changed with ease. Graphics and other elements are added in the same way. The program then turns your design on the screen into the corresponding HTML code.

The huge advantage of this system is that you know exactly what the finished page will look like before it is tested using a browser. Since HTML is something less than precise, there could be small discrepancies between the layout in the web creation program and the one produced by the browser. Any differences should be quite minor though, and easily remedied. Figure 1.41 shows a dummy web page design as it appeared in the design view of Dreamweaver, and Figure 1.42 shows the page displayed using Internet Explorer.

The original layout has been produced quite accurately, and the change in background colour is due to the design view in Dreamweaver having

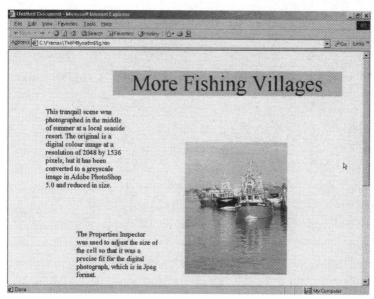

Fig.1.42 The layout as it appears in a browser

lines to aid the positioning of elements rather than a true WYSIWYG background. This type of thing is the norm with WYSIWYG page creation programs, and WYSIWYG programs in general. It is of no real consequence, but if required, many programs can be switched to something closer to a true WYSIWYG display. Fusion is one of the most WYSIWYG of WYSIWYG web page creation programs, and the layout of Figure 1.43 is very close to the version displayed by a browser (Figure 1.44), but the latter is still slightly "cleaner" than the view shown in Fusion.

Many of those who have learned HTML tend to look down on those who produce web pages using a WYSIWYG program. This is perhaps understandable, but producing web pages should be about design and getting your ideas into web print, and not about clever HTML coding and programming. A WYSIWYG page creation program enables you to start work straight away on building a sophisticated web site, which is certainly not possible if you produce all the code manually. It also enables pages to be produced quite quickly, and makes it easy to turn the pages into a coherent site. Manually producing all the HTML code and then getting everything to work together as a proper site is very time consuming.

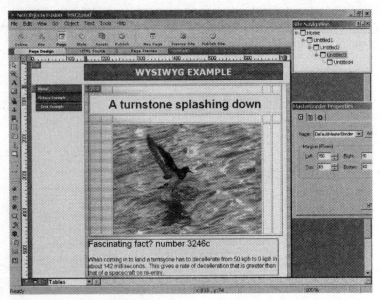

Fig.1.43 A dummy page in Fusion

Unless you have masses of spare time that can be devoted to building your web site, web publishing or a WYSWIG page creation program are the only practical options.

Uploading

Having created you new web site there is the minor matter of uploading it to the server. A few important pieces of information are needed in order to gain access to your web space, but the provider of the web space should supply this information. Without it the web space is unusable. The site is normally uploaded using FTP (file transfer protocol), and at one time it was essential to have an FTP program to handle the transfer. Several free programs of this type are available, so additional expense can be avoided if you have to use this method. Figure 1.45 shows the popular WS_FTP LE program in operation.

These days many web creation programs have built-in facilities for uploading sites, and it is probably best to use this facility if it is available. There are usually facilities that make it easy to keep sites up-to-date. In

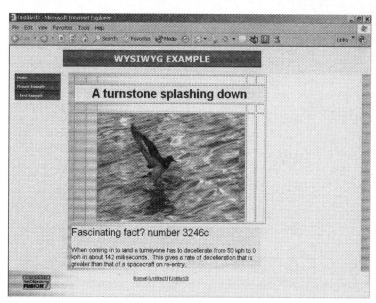

Fig.1.44 The slightly "cleaner" version displayed by a browser is very close to the version displayed in Fusion

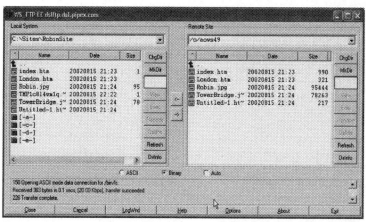

Fig.1.45 A site can be uploaded and maintained using an FTP program such as WS_FTP LE

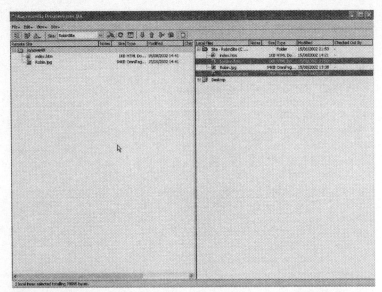

Fig.1.46 The two highlighted files on the right must be uploaded

Figure 1.46 Dreamweaver is being used to update a small site. The left-
hand section of the window shows the existing files in the site, and the
right-hand side shows the files in the new version of the site. The
highlighted files are the new or altered ones that must be uploaded.
Keeping a site up-to-date with the local site on your PC is known as
synchronisation, and with many programs it requires little more than
operating the appropriate button.

Points to remember

Look at a selection of sites and examine the contents of each page. There will be blocks of text, links, images, navigation panels, and so on. These are the basic building blocks that you will use to put together a site, and you need to know how to use and deal with each of them.

Most sites fall into broad categories, such as personal and small business sites. Decide on the size and type of site you will be building early in the proceedings, because decisions later on will have to be based on these factors. Some types of web hosting do not permit any form of commercial site for example, and there is no point in trying to build a huge site with a program intended for producing single page sites.

Web pages are written using HTML, which uses embedded codes to format text, position images, and so on. It is possible to produce web pages using nothing more than a simple text editor, but you have to learn HTML first. There are HTML editors that make it easier to produce web pages using manually generated code, but you still need to have a good understanding of HTML coding.

The quicker and easier approach to web page production is to use a WYSIWYG page creation program. These enable pages to be produced in much the same way as using a desktop publishing program, and little or no knowledge of HTML is required.

Links to other sites are optional, but for anything other than a single page site it is essential to have links that enable users to move easily from one page of the site to another. Ideally it should be possible to move directly from any page of the site to any other page. Unless you are building a large site there should be no difficulty in arranging things this way.

Links are not limited to text as the source, and images can also be used as links to other pages or sites. In fact links can use part of an image as the source, and there can be several of these "hotspots" per image if required.

Anchors can be used in long pages to permit links to target a particular part of a page. Anchors are often used in conjunction with a navigation panel at the top of the page that enables users to instantly jump to the required part of the page. Another use is to provide a quick means of going from the top of a page to the bottom or vice versa.

Activating a link to a multimedia file will result in that file being played, provided the PC has a suitable player program and (where appropriate) codec. Always include details of the player required and any add-ons needed to play or display any form of multimedia file. Links to anything other than a standard type of Internet file or multimedia file will result in the browser trying to download it.

These days HTML is augmented by scripts and programming languages that can provide interactivity and all sorts of clever features. These are not essential elements for most types of site and are not a good starting point. Initially it is best to settle for a relatively simple and straightforward site that works well. You can progress to a "bells and whistles" site later, should the need arise.

Having completed a site on your PC it must be uploaded to the server. This is normally done via FTP, and there are programs specifically designed for FTP uploading and downloading. However, many web page creation programs now have built-in facilities for uploading sites and keeping them up-to-date.

Design
matters

Look and learn

Even for those who are used to producing newsletters, books, or whatever, producing their first web site can be a daunting task. Having learned the necessary technical skills, actually designing the site will not be like anything they have tackled before. The task is even more daunting for those with no previous experience of producing any type of publication. As with any creative skill, it is generally better to "learn to walk before you can crawl". Spend some time producing a few dummy pages or even a couple of dummy sites before progressing to the real thing. This way you will have a chance to iron out any technical problems in addition to gaining valuable experience at the creative side of things.

It is particularly important not to dive straight in if you are producing a commercial site. Should the end result be artistically and technically challenged it could significantly damage the prospects of your company rather than enhance them. In fairness to users you should avoid the temptation to get your first site onto the Internet as quickly as possible. A site should be thoroughly checked before it is published on the Internet, and checked again once it has been published. Any problems should be rectified as soon as possible.

Grand tour

The best advice for beginners is to do a tour of the Internet looking at a cross section of sites. Then look at sites of a similar type to the one you intend to build. Initially, do not bother too much with the content, but instead look more at the way each site is presented, the layouts of the pages, and the layout of each site as a whole. What do you like about some sites and dislike about others? If you find a site informative and easy to use it is likely that others will find it equally user-friendly. Sites that you find awkward or even impossible to use are probably not going to be any easier for anyone else.

Any decent search engine should turn up a few sites that have links to so-called "worst of the web" sites. It can be informative to look at some of these. Many use odd colour schemes that are hard on the eye or render important elements of the site virtually invisible. There will probably be a selection of link problems, such as links that simply reload the current page, lead to nowhere, or just take you round in circles. The latter is one of the most common faults, with links that should take you to more detailed information just taking you through some superficial information and back to where you started.

Probably the best of the worst are the sites that a beautifully produced and laid out, but after several minutes of going through pages you still have no idea what the site is about! Particularly if your site is about something unusual or esoteric, it is essential for the homepage to state the subject and purpose of the site as plainly as possible. If the site is for a knowledgeable few and not for beginners it is as well to say so in large letters on the homepage.

Initially you have to make decisions about the general layout of pages and the site as a whole, but eventually you will have to fill the pages with well-written material if the site is to succeed. Remember that the purpose of the site is to convey information to visitors, and not to make you look clever. With a specialist site there will inevitably be a certain amount of jargon, but try not to get carried away. With any type of writing, plain language generally works better than text that is largely comprised of technical terms and obscure words. The simple and direct approach is even more important when producing material for the Internet, where it is likely that many visitors will not have English as their first language. The more simple the language, the more they are likely to understand.

Purpose

One of the most important things when designing a web site, and perhaps the most important thing, is to ensure that it has a sense of purpose. In other words, it should be about something. If a web site is about you, it should contain details of your life and experiences. It is very easy to wander off the point with the site actually being about your favourite pop star, the football club you follow, and your pet dog. With any web site it is easy to get sidetracked to the point that the site is no longer about

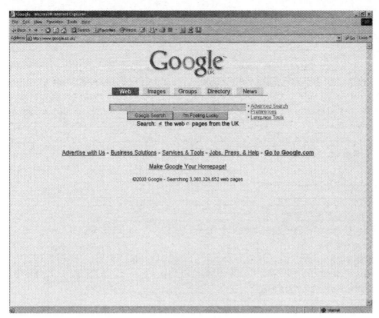

Fig.2.1 The Google sites use the minimalist approach

whatever it was originally supposed to be about. It is easy to end up with a rambling site that is not really about anything at all. Many of the beautifully produced but incomprehensible sites mentioned previously have fallen into the trap of having numerous pages with no overall theme. If the site really has to cover a number of subjects, make sure that each page has a heading that clearly states what it is about. Try to keep the site reasonably compact and focussed.

Minimalism

I think it is important to make the point that a good site does not necessarily have to use all the latest Internet tricks, have complex and cleverly designed colour schemes, etc. Many successful web sites have quite simple layouts, minimal use of colour, and a complete lack of animation, sound, rollovers, and the like. The most successful sites of recent years are those owned by the Google search engine company, and Figure 2.1 shows the homepage of the google.co.uk site. The first thing you notice about this site is that it is barely there! It is one of the

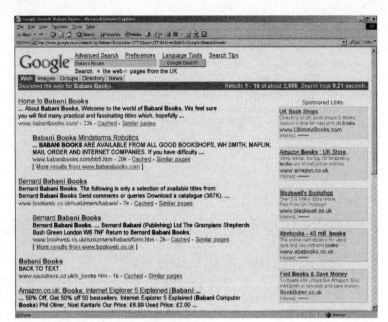

Fig.2.2   *The simple and straightforward approach is maintained when
the results are displayed*

most minimalist sites you will find, but along with the other Google sites
it is used by millions of people every day.

The Google search engine is apparently based on about 10,000 cheap
PCs in a network, which sounds like something invented by Heath
Robinson but it actually operates very quickly. The speed is helped by
the fact that the Google web pages are extremely basic and little data
per page has to be downloaded by users. Visitors to the Google sites
require quick results and are not interested in a site that looks pretty.
The Google search engine is very quick and efficient at finding results,
and it is also good at sorting them so that the results that are most likely
to be of interest are shown first.

The minimalist approach continues when the results are displayed. The
results are shown in the main body of the page with advertisements
linked to the search criteria displayed down the right-hand side of the
page (Figure 2.2). The advertisements are pretty basic though, with no
rollovers, flashing colours, or other web gizmos. This helps to keep
download times very short.

Google is about efficiency. People visiting the site require quick results, and that is what they get. The site is simple and easy to use, and no one is bothered about the lack of colour, sound, graphic effects, and so one. Users get the results they require quickly and with a minimum of fuss, so they keep coming back to the site. This brutally efficient approach might not be applicable to all types of site, but if a minimalist site quickly tells people what they need to know, it has to be regarded as a good site despite the lack of artistic flair. If a site is visually attractive, has plenty of tricks, but no one can find what they are looking for, it is definitely a bad site.

There has been a trend away from the more "jazzy" approach to sites, but I suppose the Internet would be a much duller place if all sites were to pursue this policy. If your design abilities are strictly limited it would make sense to opt for a streamlined site that looks businesslike and works well rather than a showy site that slightly misses the mark. If you have some flair for design and the subject matter of the site suits a more flamboyant approach, then this is clearly the route to take.

Colour conscious

Colour is an important consideration for web sites, and it is probably the first thing that is noticed by new visitors to a site. It is a bit like interior decorating, where the mood of a room is set by the colour scheme. The colours will set the mood of your site, and they can be bright to make a site lively or more restrained for a site that has more serious content. Bright yellows, reds, and oranges would not be appropriate for a site about dealing with bereavement, or a site that carried news stories that were frequently of a tragic nature.

Pastel shades might not be appropriate for a site about Pop Art, but on the other hand, they would help to make the bright colours in the works of art stand out from the page. On looking through several Pop Art sites, I found that they actually had some of the most sombre colour schemes on the Internet. This was presumably done as a deliberate ploy to make the pictures stand out better. You need to give some thought to the colour scheme, look at sites of a similar type to your proposed site, and avoid the temptation to jump at the obvious. The obvious will not necessarily be the right type of colour scheme for your new site, and you might be able to come up with something that works better.

Colour needs to be sympathetic to the type of site you are producing, but above all else it needs to be practical. Probably the most common

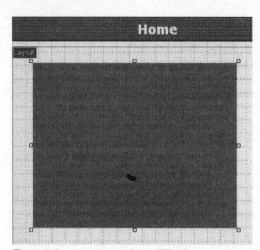

Fig.2.3 Low contrast gives difficult to read text

mistake is to use foreground and background colours for text that leave it virtually unreadable. Bright colours, particularly when used for the background colour, are unlikely to give text that is easy to read. The most important thing is to have plenty of contrast between the foreground and background colours. On most monitors dark text on a light background displays more clearly than light text on a dark background, but either should produce text that is reasonably easy to read. A lack of contrast more or less guarantees that users will have to strain their eyes in order to read the text, as in the two examples of Figures 2.3 and 2.4. These examples are in greyscale, but using colour makes remarkably little difference. Contrasting colours, even without a light/ dark contrast, might be expected to produce readable text. In practice they are very unlikely to do so, and a contrast of tone is essential.

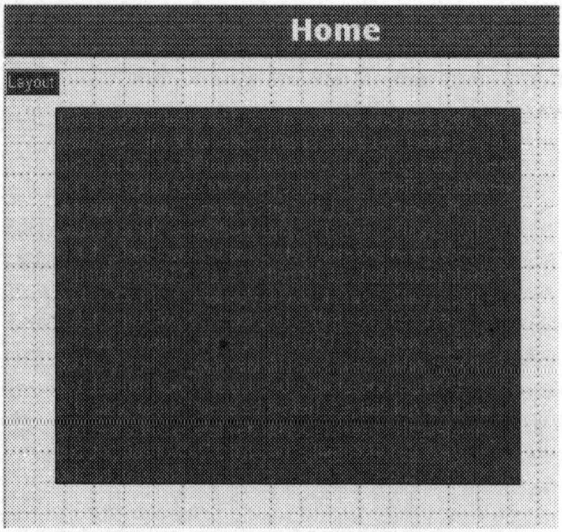

*Fig.2.4 Light text on a dark background with
low contrast works no better*

Bear in mind that a small but significant

proportion of visitors to your site will suffer from red-green colour-blindness. Red text on a green background (or vice versa) is not considered a good combination, because the two colours will appear the same to some afflicted with colour-blindness. Actually, provided there is a suitable contrast in tone the text should still be readable by someone with this condition, but it is probably best to err on the side of caution and avoid this combination.

Avoid using too many colours on web pages. It is not necessarily wrong to use more than (say) two or three colours for the text, and another two or three for the backgrounds. However, the more colours that are used, the harder it becomes get the pages to look really good. The more colours used, the easier it is to produce pages that look like they have been designed by an overenthusiastic five year old. If you look at some professionally designed web sites you will probably find that most of them use a very limited range of colours.

Consistent approach

It might seem like a good idea to have a different background colour for each page, or even a completely different colour scheme for each page. Users tend to be happier with a consistent approach to site design, where moving on to another page does not give the impression that they have accidentally moved on to another site. With a large site a different colour scheme could be used for each section of the site, but it is generally best to go for consistency. For most sites the best approach is to use the same style and colour scheme throughout.

Bright colours can be attention grabbing, but only if used in the right way. A common mistake is to use bright colours in abundance, but how do you make something attention grabbing when it is in a page full of bright colours? In the Pop Art example given earlier the sites use restrained background colours to make the photographs of artworks stand out from the page and grab your attention. The same basic approach can be used to make practically any element or set of elements the centre of attention. Obviously some images will lack bright colours, but they can be placed on what are otherwise greyscale pages, or given a border having a strong colour. Either way they should stand out nicely from the other subject matter.

Text size

Colour is not the only consideration when dealing with text. Another point to bear in mind when formatting text on a web page is that small sizes can also be difficult to read when viewed using some monitors. This is not necessarily a fault with the monitor, and it can simply be due to large monitors operating at high resolutions. A web page designed to fit a relatively low resolution screen will be displayed quite small on a high resolution monitor, perhaps using less than half the width of the screen. This effectively reduces a 19-inch monitor to a 9-inch type, making text at the standard size quite small. Text in the smaller sizes could be virtually unreadable on this type of screen. In fact the small text sizes tend to be difficult to read on most monitors.

It is tempting to use small text sizes when dealing with large amounts of text. Small text enables large amounts to be crammed onto each page, but a mass of tiny text is unlikely to be popular with users of your site. Use the smaller text sizes very sparingly, and never use anything smaller than the standard size for large amounts of written material. It is probably best to avoid having really large documents on a web site except in downloadable form, such as a PDF file. Those who are interested can then download the file and view it at their leisure. Files of this type can be viewed at full size using any screen resolution, and in most cases it is possible to produce high quality printouts from them if users prefer to read the material in this form.

Fonts

Users of word processors and desktop publishing programs often use all sorts of exotic fonts in their publications, but unusual fonts do not necessarily work well when applied to web pages. In fact they often work quite badly. One problem is that a font installed on your PC may not be present on all the computers used to access your site. Where necessary, the browser programs will substitute what are supposed to be suitable equivalents, but there is no guarantee that substitute fonts will be even vaguely similar to the originals.

In addition to the fact that the text will often be displayed in an unsuitable font, it might take up too much or too little space. This can happen anyway, and the appearance of pages will often differ slightly from one browser to another. Differences in screen resolution can also produce variations in the appearance of a page. Any additional changes due to the substitution of an inappropriate font are unwelcome. If you really must have a headline in an unusual font, the best approach is probably to generate it as a graphic file and then add it to the page like any other image. Because it is an image it does not require users to have the appropriate font installed on their PC. Glowing text, "metallic" text, etc., can be added via the same route. One slight disadvantage of this approach is that it increases the amount of data that has to be downloaded, so it is best not to have too many headings of this type per page.

It is as well to bear in mind that text displayed on a monitor is generally less easy to read than printed text. For web use many designers prefer to use simple fonts such as Arial and Helvetica rather than types that have serifs. Some consider that serifs make small text easier to read, but as already pointed out, it is best not to use much text that is smaller than the base size. There is really no excuse for producing hard to read text because all web pages should be tested in a browser before a site is published, and any problem with the text should "stick out like a sore thumb".

Headings

Use plenty of headings and subheadings to break up large pieces of text. In general, it is best to keep web content as brief and to the point as possible, with more subheadings than would be used in equivalent material for the printed page. The extra subheadings are not used simply to make the pages look prettier, although when used sensibly they will probably have that effect. People surfing the web are often in a hurry, and will probably not bother to wade through masses of text to see if a page has the information that they require. Well written subheadings and economically written text help users to quickly assess the relevance of a page, and locate the information they require if it is actually there.

Try to give the text a structure and do not simply add subheadings randomly. Headings and subheadings are generally arranged with a large heading at the top, smaller subheadings for each main topic, and possibly yet smaller subheadings for each topic within the main blocks of text. The smallest subheadings are still at least equal to the size of the body text, and are typically a little larger. Headings and subheadings are usually in bold print so that they stand out from the main text. Different colours can also be used to make them stand out from the main text, but using bold print alone is sufficient.

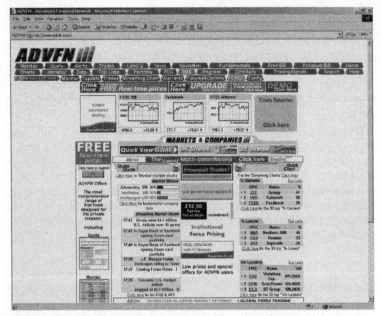

Fig.2.5 The ADVFN site has a navigation bar near the top of the screen

It is not a good idea to underline headings, subheadings, or indeed any text. Links are usually indicated by being in a different colour and by being underlined. Underlining text can confuse users by making them think that the text is a link. It is particularly important not to underline any headings or subheadings that are in a different colour to the main text, as this would make them look just like links. Blue is often used for link text, so be especially careful when using blue text. Using bold text, italics, or even a different font is a safer way of emphasising small pieces of text.

Hyperlinks

The Internet relies very heavily on hyperlinks, or just plain "links" as they are generally called these days. How many people would bother to surf the Internet if the full URL had to be typed in for every page that was visited? Probably very few people and the Internet would certainly not have achieved its current level of success without links. You need links to permit users to move from one page of your site to another. Ideally it should be possible to reach any page of the site from any other page of

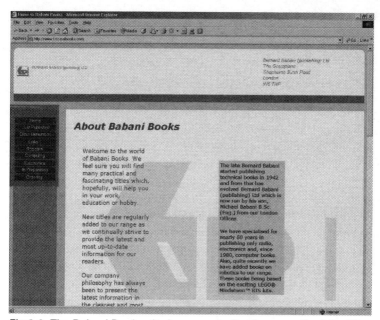

*Fig.2.6 The Babani Books site has a navigation frame on the left with
the content frame to the right*

the site. With smallish sites this is not usually a problem, and the normal
method is to have a link to each page via a menu bar at the top of the
page or a set of buttons down the left-hand side of each page. The
ADVFN site (Figure 2.5) has a number of buttons near the top of the
window that access various parts of the site.

As another example, the Babani Books site has the set of buttons on the
left-hand side of the page (Figure 2.6), which is probably the most popular
layout. This method works best when used with frames, because the
buttons then remain stationary if the frame containing the main content
is scrolled. The same is true if the buttons are positioned at the top of
the window, or anywhere else for that matter. You need to seriously
consider the use of frames with any layout of this general type.

With large sites it is not practical to have one button per page. One way
around this is to have a few buttons, with each one leading into another
page that has a further set of buttons. In effect, the site is divided into
several sub-sites that are accessed from the homepage. Many of the
buttons on the ADVFN homepage actually lead to sub-sites rather than

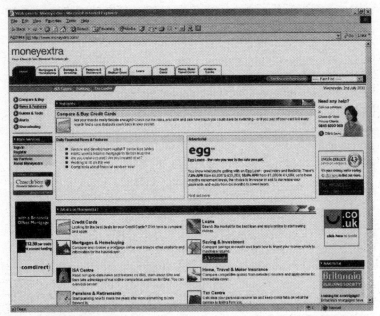

Fig.2.7 The MoneyXtra site has a menu near the top left-hand corner
of the screen

single pages. Another method is the guided tour approach. This has
the usual buttons on the homepage, but all or some of these buttons
lead into a series of pages that gradually give users more and more
information about a certain topic. There is nothing innately wrong with
the guided tour approach, but it is something that is not often implemented
well. Many sites that use this method take a lot of pages to tell you very
little, and never really get to the point. Some just send you round in
circles. For many web users it is a case of "once bitten, twice shy".
There is a risk that most visitors to the site will go elsewhere instead of
going through the tours.

Another method is to have a sophisticated menu system that includes
drop-down menus. With (say) ten menus each having ten entries the
system would provide access to one hundred pages. This is another
method that requires the site to be divided into what are effectively sub-
sites, with each menu covering one section of the site. One way of
navigating the MoneyXtra site (Figure 2.7) is to use the menu system
near the top left-hand corner of the window.

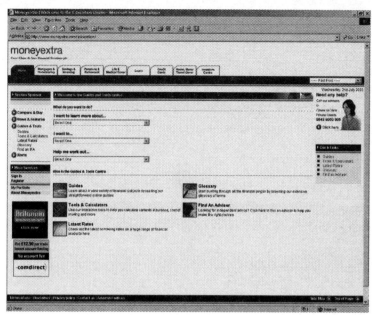

Fig.2.8 Activating an entry expands it to show the available options

Operating one of the entries in this menu expands it (Figure 2.8) so that links to a number of pages are shown. The contents of the main frame change to suit the selected topic. Operating a different entry in the main menu contracts the original entry and expands the new one (Figure 2.9). Again, the contents of the main frame alter to suit the newly selected topic. It is not actually that difficult to produce drop-down menus and other complex menu systems using one of the more upmarket page creation programs, but for beginners it is probably best to keep things simple initially and settle for a few pages accessed via a set of buttons. There are plenty of clever gizmos available if you need them later.

Missing link

It is important to thoroughly check completed web sites, and this is not just a matter of checking the site before it is published on the Internet. Check all the links once it has been uploaded, and it is not a bad idea to make periodic checks thereafter. Web pages have been known to go "absent without leave". In fact whole web sites have been known to

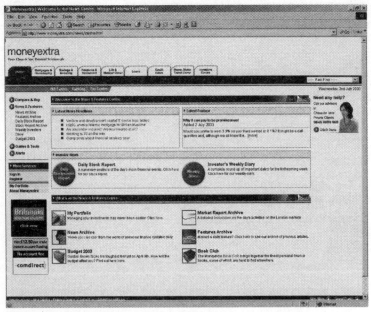

Fig.2.9 A different category can be selected and expanded

disappear from servers, but a problem on this scale will presumably be noticed fairly early in the proceedings. Things like missing pages and images will probably not be noticed unless you go looking for them. Also, make a full check of the links after making any modifications to your site. Some web creation programs will automatically sort out the links when changes are made to pages, but in most cases at least some input from the user is required in order to sort things out.

Incorrect links to other web sites are probably the main cause of link related problems. Links to other sites can be liberally scattered through the text, but it is more practical to have the links in their own frame or even on their own page. This makes it easy to check them and make any necessary changes. It is easy to make mistakes when typing long web addresses, but the copy and paste method can be used to avoid errors. Go to the web page using a browser such as Internet Explorer, and then left-click the text in the address bar to select it. Next press Control – C to copy the text, and the go back to the web creation program. Either use Control – Z or the Paste option from the menu system to copy the address into the web creation program. Make sure the text cursor is in the correct place prior to pasting the address onto the page.

Providing links to other sites might not seem like a very bright thing to do, as it is making it easy for visitors to move on from your site. Indeed, it is actively encouraging them to do so. However, it is links that make the Internet work, and it would soon decline in popularity if most site designers declined to include links to other sites. Provided your site is well produced and interesting, visitors will stay a while before moving on, and they will probably return at some time in the future. If your site is badly produced and boring, visitors will soon hit the Back button and will not return. Quality of content and presentation is the only way to get people to use your site and keep using it.

Before adding links to other sites it is normal to contact the administrators of the sites to ensure that they have no objections. With luck they will reciprocate and add links from their sites to yours. Sites often come, go, move, or suspend operations for a while. It is important to check links to other sites quite frequently and make any necessary alterations. If users try a couple of links and they do not work it is likely that they will conclude that your site is old and out of date. They will then exit the site and will probably never return. One of the main attractions of the web for most users is its freshness and immediacy. Any hint of staleness will probably make users leave your site for good.

Music

It is tempting to add sound to your site as it is a good way to grab peoples' attention. Unfortunately, in grabbing their attention it is quite likely to annoy them as well. Even with something like a site devoted to a certain type of music, most visitors would prefer to have music only on demand. Remember that most music is protected by copyright, and that it is illegal to use it without permission and, where appropriate, paying the necessary fee. It is possible to buy CDs that contain copyright-free music that you can use on web sites, in your home movies, or whatever. The quality of this music is not usually very good artistically or technically, but one of the better CDs might suit your requirements. In general it is best not to bother with sound on web sites unless there is a very good reason to do so.

Images

Sound might not be a particularly desirable feature for most web sites, but images certainly are. The old adage that "a picture is worth a thousand words" is probably more apt in an Internet context than in any other. The problem in using lots of small images or a few large ones is that the amount of data required to produce each page becomes quite large. This gives long download times. Use lots of large images and the download times can become very long indeed.

The speed problem can be minimised by making the images no larger than is absolutely necessary, and by using compression to further reduce file sizes. Editing images for web use is covered in chapter 4, so it will not be considered any further here. Even with well processed images it is still not practical to use several large images per page, because the download time would still be far too long for those with 56k Internet connections. A few images of modest size spread through the text works very well, so this is not really a major problem. If you are producing a photo album rather than a normal web site, the usual approach is to have small thumbnail images that act as links to larger versions of the images. This gives a quick download time for each page and avoids having users wait while images that are of no interest are downloaded.

Download time

Download times are an important consideration when designing web pages. Large amounts of text do not produce massive amounts of data, with about one kilobyte being sufficient to accommodate about 170 words. A couple of thousand words, which is a large amount for a web page, would therefore come to about 12 kilobytes of data. With a 56k modem this gives a download time of two or three seconds. A typical web image has a file size of about 10 to 70 kilobytes. Pages that contain few words but many images might look quite attractive, but a fair proportion of users could be left waiting two or three minutes while each page downloads.

Where it is important to use numerous images it is advisable to split them across several pages. This gives several short download times rather than one long download, which most users find more tolerable. An alternative approach is to use the photo album method mentioned previously, with a small image acting as a link to a larger version of the image file. It is an approach that is equally valid in a non-photo album context, and it is particularly useful if a more detailed image will be of real help to visitors. It is also a good approach if some of the photographs are spectacular and look at their best when viewed large.

The thumbnail images are each quite small in terms of data, so even with half a dozen or so the download time for a page should be reasonably short. Users only need to download full-size images that are of interest, so they do not waste time downloading pictures that they will not bother to look at properly, or images that are of no interest at all. Making them wait an eternity for images to download will not make you popular with visitors to your site. If, after the wait, the images are not what they are looking for, they will probably be a bit annoyed and exit the site immediately.

It is tempting to have a large and impressive homepage, but a small and impressive homepage is better. Many web users are not prepared to wait more than a few seconds for the initial page to download, so it is important that the homepage is kept reasonably compact. Unless a single-page site is being built, the normal approach is for the homepage to give a quick introduction and act as a portal to other pages where the main content is provided. With this arrangement it should not be difficult to keep the size of the homepage within reason. Unless you are building a site that is genuinely small it is not a good idea to opt for a single-page site, where the single page would probably have a very long download time. Breaking the site up into an introductory homepage and two or three support pages usually works better.

Pop-ups

Pop-up windows are, to say the least, not very popular with Internet users. It sometimes seems as if every web page you visit produces one or two pop-ups. Some sites have been known to produce so many pop-ups that visitors' PCs do not have sufficient memory to accommodate all the copies of the browser that are launched. This is not to say that pop-up windows should not be used at all. With an online photo-album for example, it is a perfectly valid approach to have the selected photograph pop-up in its own window. The user can close that window when they have finished viewing the photograph, select another one, close that window, and so on. They also have the option of leaving a window open while moving on to another photograph. This makes it easy to go back to the photograph if required, or compare it to one of the others.

The kind of pop-up that most users object to is the type that pops up automatically when a page is accessed. Many of these carry advertisements that support the site, and your site may well have these if it is hosted by a free web hosting company or you use hosting that is subsidised by advertising. Where the choice is available, most people opt for banner advertising rather than the dreaded pop-ups. It is probably worth paying a little extra to get rid of the advertisements altogether.

Some sites have pop-up windows as a proper part of the site rather than to provide advertising revenue. Although it might seem like a good way of making your site more lively and interesting, if you are not careful it can easily become confusing and an annoyance. Also, it is likely that most users will close the pop-up window before it is fully loaded. Consequently, rather than drawing their attention to something important, the pop-up would probably result in them never seeing it. The general feeling towards automatic pop-ups is such that it is probably best not to use them at all.

Missing material

Deciding what should be included on a web site and what should be omitted can be difficult. It is often helpful to make a list of everything you would like to include and then sort the list according to the importance of each item, starting with the most important at the top. Try to make sure that everything in the top two thirds of the list is included. Include the rest if you can do so without making the site excessively large or too boring.

With a commercial site it is important to make sure that important information such as contact details and prices are included. A good way of checking the site is to try it out as a dummy customer. You should try to look at things from the customer's point of view when designing the site, but it is easy to make silly mistakes and miss out important information. If you try out the site, using it in the same way as your customers, you should find any real "clangers" before any harm is done. Try to find specific items of information, check Email links to ensure that the messages get through. Even some quite large sites have been published without any contact information being included, so make sure that any contact numbers, etc., are included. It is a good idea to have a page or pages specifically for contact information, terms of business, etc.

If you place an advertisement in a magazine or newspaper inviting people to visit the web site for more information, make sure that the site does actually include more information. It is not uncommon for people to be directed to a web site where all they find is the same advertisement that appeared in the magazine or newspaper. Wasting the time of potential customers is likely to ensure that they remain just that. Do not advertise your web site until it has actually been published. At the height of the Internet boom there were a surprisingly large number of sites advertised

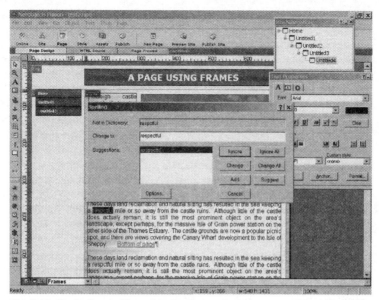

Fig.2.10 Fusion's spelling checker is much the same as the equivalent feature of a word processor

that either failed to appear for months, or never appeared at all. A non-existent commercial web site will give potential customers the impression that your company has gone "belly up".

Spelling

It is not the end of the world if a web site has one or two spelling errors or faults in the grammar. No one is perfect, and visitors to your site will mostly be quite happy to tolerate the odd error here and there, especially if the site provides the information that they require. Numerous errors are another matter. They can make the material difficult to follow and can produce vague or even misleading text. In the case of a commercial site anything more than the occasional error will definitely give visitors the impression that your company is incompetent and unreliable.

With large amounts of text it is definitely a good idea to produce the material on a good word processor such as Microsoft Word, making use of the grammar and spelling checkers. The finished piece can then be imported into a page creation program or copied and pasted from one program to the other. The grammar checkers in Word and other word processors are by no means perfect, but they will sometimes spot errors. It is helpful to get someone else to read through the text in search of mistakes. A fresh pair of eyes will often spot one or two glaring errors that you somehow managed to miss. If your PC has a text to speech facility, get this to speak the text. Errors missed when reading through the text are often pretty obvious when you hear the text being spoken.

Spelling checkers are very efficient, but they simply check each word in your text against a dictionary of words. Anything in your text that is not in the dictionary will be brought to your attention. Names and obscure technical terms will usually be picked up by the spelling checker even though they are correct, but an incorrect spelling that that just happens to match another word in the dictionary will get through. If you type "smelling" instead of "spelling" for example, or "though" instead of "through", it will not be picked up by the spelling checker. Therefore, careful manual checking is still very important.

With small amounts of text most people prefer to type the words straight into the page creation program. Manual checking should be sufficient with small amounts of material, but most of the better web page creation programs have built-in spelling checkers. Figure 2.10 shows the spelling checker of Netobjects Fusion spotting the deliberate mistake. It has the usual spelling checker features and is used in precisely the same fashion as the equivalent facility of a word processor. A single page or the complete site can be checked. It is a good idea to give all the text a final check if a spelling checker is available. You might have accidentally damaged some text while making up the pages.

Style

On the face of it, writing for the web is no different from writing for any other medium such as a magazine or book. It is not really as simple as that, and there is no universal style anyway. Material written for a book would be handled differently to material on the same subject but for a magazine article. For a start, the book would be much larger than the magazine article, and it could therefore cover the subject in far greater depth. As already explained, text on a computer monitor is generally harder to read than printed text, so there is good reason to keep pieces of text for web use as short as possible. This also helps to avoid excessively large pages and sites.

Also as pointed out previously, large amounts of text can be stored on the site as downloadable Microsoft Word DOC or Adobe PDF files which

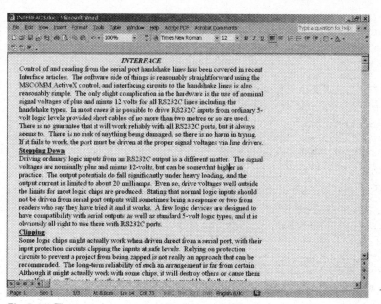

Fig.2.11 The test document as it appears in Word

users can download and print out. If you have no means of making a DOC or PDF file, any text editor or word processor can produce a basic text file (txt) format file. Little formatting can be included in a text file, but a basic text file will produce good quality text when printed out. If necessary, users can load a text file into a word processor and alter the font, text size, or any other aspect of the formatting, prior to printing the document.

There are free programs and web sites that can be used to produce PDF files. Ghostscript is the best known free PDF program, and there is an interesting alternative in the form of PDF995. This is apparently based on Ghostscript, but it handles things in a more user-friendly fashion. Figure 2.11 shows some formatted text in word, and in order to convert it to a PDF file using PDF995 it is just a matter of selecting the Print option from the file menu, and then selecting PDF995 as the printer (Figure 2.12). You then go ahead and print the document to a file, and this file is the required PDF type. Figure 2.13 shows the converted document displayed in Adobe Acrobat, and the formatting has been retained quite well.

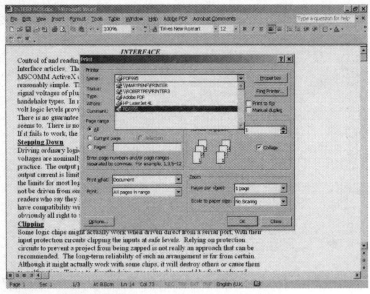

Fig.2.12 PDF995 operates as a sort of virtual printer

In most cases it is possible to avoid huge amounts of text that do not fit well into a few web pages. People using the Internet are generally in a hurry, and the main reason that they use the Internet is that it is perceived as the quickest way of finding out what they need to know. Having written a piece for a web page, go back through it and make it even more brief and to the point. Remember to use plenty of helpful subheadings so that people can quickly locate the information they require. Witty subheadings that do not really give any clues about the associated text are probably out of place on a web page.

The two list facilities of HTML are not there simply to provide a means of making pages look more attractive. Lists can be used as a means of quickly conveying important information to the reader. As with many features, it is something that generally works best when used sparingly. Lists are not normally used as an alternative to explanatory text, and it will usually be necessary to follow each list with at least a few brief explanations of the points made in the list.

Another useful ploy is to have a wide margin that contains summaries of the points covered in the main text. Like headings and lists, this enables

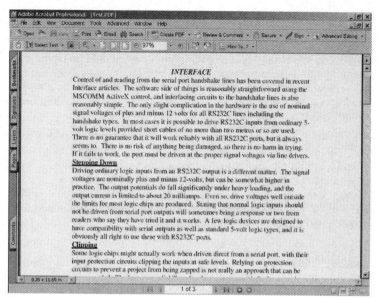

Fig.2.13 The PDF version of the document

visitors to quickly locate the information they require, or move on to another page if the information is not there. Most people prefer to have the text in manageable chunks, so break up long pieces of text into several pages. Next and Previous links can be used to make it easy to go back and forth through the pages.

Under construction

At one time it seemed as though there were no completed sites on the Internet, and practically every site had a sign saying "Under construction" or something similar. Half finished and semi-working sites are pretty useless, and will usually have surfers exiting as quickly as possible. The lessons of the past have now been largely learnt, and the vast majority of sites are fully working. Avoid the temptation to publish a site that is not complete. It will generate a lot of bad feeling and half a site is unlikely to be of any real use to anyone.

Most sites tend to grow over the years, and in a sense just about every web site is under construction. You can publish a small site first and gradually add to it, and this is a good way of doing things. Each published version of the site should be finished and fully operational though. It is all right to point out that more pages will be added later, but the pages in the existing site should be complete and the site should be useful as it stands. There should definitely not be any links to pages that have not been added yet. Do not promise to add features unless you are sure that you can "deliver the goods". Expect a lot of Emails of complaint if you let people down.

If you find that your site has been in a semi-finished state for a long time it is likely that you have "bitten off more than you can chew". It is better to have a less ambitious site that is finished and published on the Internet rather than one which always being constructed but is never actually finished. It is very easy to get carried away when embarking on your first web site. Try to take a down-to-earth attitude to site production and concentrate on quality rather than quantity.

Clear idea

Before embarking on the construction of your first site it is advisable to try out a few ideas using your chosen page creation program. Try to become reasonably fluent with the program before starting work with it in earnest. When making initial experiments with page construction and design it does not matter too much if you dabble, with no clear idea of what the finished page will look like. The situation is different when you start to produce the real thing. You need to have a clear idea of the site's layout, and the layout of each page.

You also need to know the content for each page. Large amounts of text should be prepared using a word processor prior to starting work with the page creation program. The text can be imported into the page creation program or copied and pasted into it. Any images or other files should also be prepared and ready for use before you start making up the pages. Unless the site is very small it will be necessary to make some notes and (or) produce a simple chart showing the general arrangement of the site and each page within it.

It is important to have a plan for the site, but it is equally important to be flexible in your approach. When the pages are produced it is likely that some will be much longer or shorter than expected. A colour scheme that seemed like a good idea at the time might not live up to expectations. If necessary, merge two pages into one, split one page into two, try a different colour scheme, or whatever. If a page looks right and works

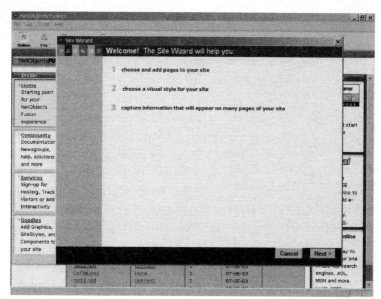

Fig.2.14 The initial page when the wizard is run

well, resist the temptation to fiddle with it in an attempt to produce even better results. Remember the old American adage, "if it ain't broke, don't fix it".

Templates

These days many web page creation programs have templates, and these can make life much easier if you do not feel confident about designing your own site from scratch. A template is effectively a ready made site that lacks any content. The basic idea is that you choose a site layout that suits your requirements, and then start adding content in the pages. You still have to provide the content, but you do not have to worry about links to permit people to navigate the site, or any of the basic structure. It is all provided for you.

Some programs provide templates for web pages. Various layouts are offered, with each one having space for a main heading, spaces for text and images, and so on. You choose the layout that best suits your needs and then add the content. This type of thing limits your creative potential,

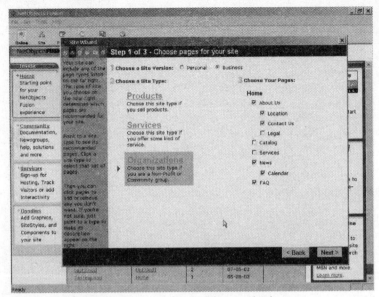

Fig.2.15 Selecting the type of site and the required pages

but for those with limited design expertise it permits quite professional looking pages to be constructed quite easily and quickly. Using templates does not guarantee good results because you still have to supply some worthwhile content for the pages, but it increases your chances of success and saves time. The template approach to site and page design is covered in the next chapter, which deals with web publishing. Although mainly associated with web publishing, it is also available when using many web page creation programs.

Wizards

The wizard approach is quite common in web publishing but it is also available when using some web page creation programs. Opting for the Site Wizard of Fusion produces the initial window of Figure 2.14, which just gives brief details of the steps involved in setting up a new site. At the next window (Figure 2.15) you choose the type of site required and the pages it will contain. Next the page layout and colour scheme are selected (Figure 2.16), and then your details or the details of your

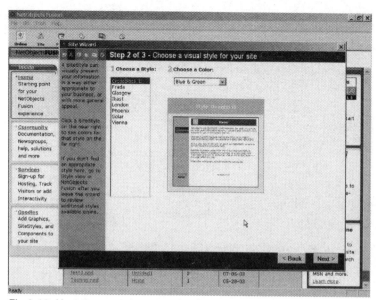

Fig.2.16 Next the page layout and colour scheme are selected

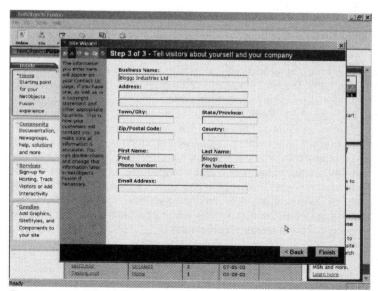

Fig.2.17 Company/personal details are entered on this form

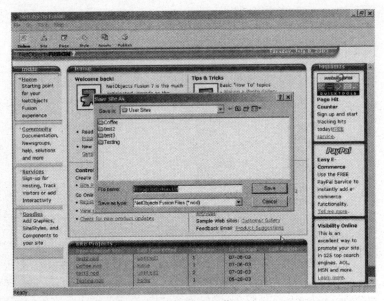

Fig.2.18 The completed site is saved to disc

company are entered into a form (Figure 2.17). This completes the process, and the site is saved to disc (Figure 2.18).

Opening the site produces a diagram showing the layout of the site (Figure 2.19). Double-clicking one of the pages in the site diagram results in the corresponding page being opened in Fusion's page view mode, as in Figure 2.20. Each page has some text that indicates the type of content that should be added, but it is obviously up to you to add most of the content. It is unlikely that either the template or wizard methods will produce a basic site that precisely matches your needs, but remember that it is usually possible to make changes and tailor the site to your exact requirements. The template and wizard approaches are particularly useful if you are having difficulty getting started. They will get you "up and running", and once under way you will probably have little difficulty in taking the site through to completion.

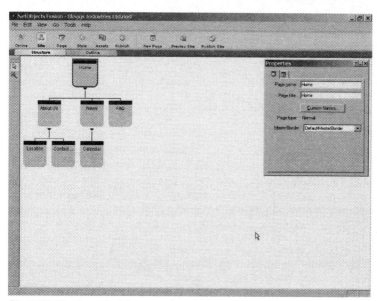

Fig.2.19 The layout of the completed site

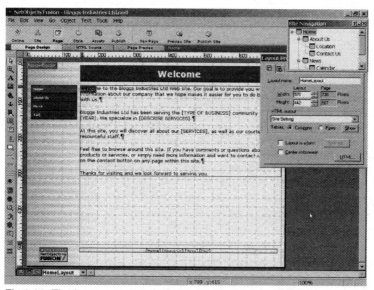

Fig.2.20 The homepage ready for the content to be added

Points to remember

You can learn a great deal by doing a tour of the Internet and casting a critical eye over the sites you visit. Look at a good selection of sites and decide what aspects of each one you like and dislike. Then look at some sites of a similar type to the one you are going to build.

It is not necessary to build a site that has all the latest gimmicks. There is nothing wrong with a simple and straightforward site that works well. Just the opposite in fact, and many professional make a good living producing precisely that type of site. An excessively jazzy site that does not work is what you have to avoid.

Using bright colours will make your site lively, but it might not work well and could be unpopular with visitors. Choose colours that make text easy to read, and this means having plenty of contrast between the background and the text. Contrast is needed in the light/dark sense, and contrasting colours alone will not make text easy to read. Using bright colours, especially for backgrounds, makes it difficult to get any text on the page to really stand out. Bright backgrounds can also help to produce eyestrain.

Use text that is smaller than the base size very sparingly, if at all. Text at the base size is actually displayed quite small on many monitors, rendering the smaller sizes very difficult to read on these monitors.

Fancy fonts that display perfectly well on your monitor might not do so when the pages are displayed using other PCs. Also, fancy fonts are often relatively difficult to read when displayed on a monitor. Using lots of fonts can give a random appearance to a page. The safe approach is to use a strictly limited number (say two or three) of simple and easy to read fonts.

Numerous long pages of text will not go down well with the average surfer, who requires quick and easy results. Be as economic as possible and use plenty of headings, lists, or margin notes to help visitors to the site find what they are looking for quickly and easily. If you must include large amounts of text, consider having them in the form of a downloadable PDF file rather than a normal part of the site.

Ideally your web site should not be a random collection of pages. Try to give it a proper structure, with things arranged logically and sensibly. This is not just a matter of making it look pretty. A well designed site is much easier to use than one that is here, there, and everywhere, with broken links and other faults.

Do not publish your site until it is finished and properly tested. You will probably wish to add pages to the site over a period of time, but the initial version should be complete as far as it goes, with no links to pages that have not been added yet. Try to keep spelling mistakes and errors in the grammar to an absolute minimum.

Have a clear idea of what the finished site will look like before you start building it, and make sure that any source files you will need are completed before you start work. Be flexible and prepared to make changes if things do not work well. Leave things as they are if they look good and do work well.

If you have difficulty getting started, consider using a template or a wizard facility to get the basic site design in place. It should then be easy to complete the site.

Hosts and web publishing

Options

Large web sites are usually installed on a dedicated server that only caters for that particular site, but this type of thing is only for the "big league" players at present. The rest of us have to find simpler and cheaper means of accommodating our sites. This means finding a company that hires web space, or gives it away free. On the face of it you can design your web site first and find a web host later or perhaps find a host while the site is under construction.

In reality this might be an acceptable way of doing things, but you could find that you are "putting the horse before the cart". Building the site first is fine if there is plenty of money available to pay for the web hosting. There is bound to be a host that has the facilities you require, albeit at a price. When working on a tight budget it might be better to find the best hosting deal and accept a few compromises when building the site.

Web hosts are divided into three broad categories, which are the free space providers, ISPs that provide free space to their customers, and companies that hire web space. All three will be considered in detail here.

Free

During the Internet boom there was a vast range of freebies on offer, and companies seemed to be reluctant to sell most kinds of service. Things such as news, financial data, competitions, and web space were all "up for grabs". In some cases the companies concerned had no intention of offering their services for free in the long term, and their free offerings were just a means of "hooking" customers prior to charging for their services. In other cases the idea was to make money from advertising with the services being free forever.

Commercial realities have resulted in far fewer Internet freebies being available in the post boom period. Free offers to entice new customers tend to run for very short periods, and many of the genuinely free services have either disappeared or they are now provided at normal commercial rates. The amount of advertising available and the rates on offer were not sufficient to fund all the free services there were on offer a few years ago. This is not to say that there are no longer any free facilities on the Internet. There are still plenty of free services such as Email and financial news, but the free offerings tend to be quite basic with more comprehensive services available to those prepared to pay extra.

This is certainly the case with web space, and you can still have a web site hosted at zero cost. As one would expect though, free web hosting has "strings attached". Free web hosting is financed by advertising revenue, and your site will therefore be accompanied by some form of advertising. This used to be in the form of so-called banner advertising. In other words, an advertisement is added into your web site, and this is normally in the form of a panel at the top of the home page. In fact this panel may well be featured on every page of the site.

These days pop-up windows are often used instead or offered as an alternative. Web pages that pop up under or over the main page have the advantage of leaving your own pages clear of advertisements, but they are not popular with Internet users. In fact they are extremely unpopular and generate a certain amount of hostility from most users. The banner approach could therefore be considered the more user-friendly, and it is perhaps the better option even if it does slightly spoil your carefully designed page layouts.

Free drawbacks

While getting your web site hosted free of charge is an attractive proposition, free web hosting has some disadvantages that have to be taken into account. There are usually some restrictions on the type of web site that can be hosted, in addition to the usual restrictions requiring sites to be legal, decent and honest. In particular, any form of commercial site is often banned by free web hosting companies. This is clearly not a problem if your proposed site is a purely personal or family site with no commercial connection whatever. On the other hand, it rules out many of the free providers if you need a site to promote or support the family business or something of this nature.

Another point to bear in mind is the amount of web space provided. Most of the free web hosts provide at least a few megabytes of storage,

which is sufficient for at least a few simple web pages. In fact it should
be sufficient for a few fairly complex pages. However, if you need to use
a large number of images, have files for people to download, add music,
etc., a few megabytes will be totally inadequate. Some free web hosts
actually provide quite large amounts of space, but the amount of space
on offer is often quite large compared to the available bandwidth. In
other words, although up to (say) 500 megabytes of storage might be
on offer, the bandwidth might be just one gigabyte (1000 megabytes per
month).

A gigabyte per month is probably more than enough for many sites, but
with a 500 megabyte site it is the equivalent of every page in the site
being uploaded just twice per month. Potentially, your site will work
properly for the first few days of each month, but for the rest of the month
users will receive a message stating that the site's bandwidth has been
exceeded. With a daily limit it will work for a few hours a day but will be
inaccessible the rest of the time.

Judging the amount of bandwidth required for a site is a difficult task,
and is probably impossible. A massive site having numerous large files
for users to download could require a massive bandwidth. On the face
of it, a small site having simple pages requires little bandwidth. However,
the large site requires only a limited bandwidth if visitors are few and far
between, and the small site requires a massive bandwidth if it has to
accommodate thousands of visitors every day.

With a family site designed to keep your family and friends in touch it is
unlikely that there will be enough visitors to make bandwidth an issue.
Bandwidth is more important if the site is about your favourite pop singer
or band, and you are trying to attract as many visitors as possible to your
business site. It is advisable to have plenty of bandwidth available if you
are after a mass market, even if it means paying for that bandwidth.

Downtime

Accessibility is another factor that has to be taken into account. This is
not just a matter of the reliability of the server, although this is something
that should also be taken into account. Probably the most common
reason for sites being inaccessible is not that the server has crashed or
developed a fault. It is more common for the problem to be one of
inadequate bandwidth at peak times. Whether you pay a modest fee for
web space or obtain it for nothing, there will not be a server dedicated to
your site. Unless you pay a significant sum of money for the privilege of

using a dedicated server, the server used for your site will also be used to host several others. This is called virtual hosting. In general, the less you pay for web hosting, the greater the number of users that will share the server used for your site.

Each user is allocated a certain amount of bandwidth, but this bandwidth will not be used up at a constant rate. Each site will have periods when there is a lot of activity and other times when there is none. In theory, having a large number of sites on one server has the advantage of spreading peak time loading, since it is likely that each site will peak at a different time of day, and on different days. In practice there will probably be times when there is a great deal of activity on several sites at once and things will then virtually grind to a halt. Another potential problem is that a fault in one site on a server can result in all of the sites on that server becoming inaccessible. The more sites per server, the greater the risk of one causing the system to crash.

As already pointed out, free web space is often for non-commercial use only. Some free web hosts do permit some types of commercial use, but is free web hosting really a good choice for a commercial site? The web addresses for free sites are often quite long, whereas a short and easy to use address is important for a commercial site. It will probably be obvious to many of your potential customers that the web site is provided by a free web host, which is not going to give the impression that your company is a solid and well established outfit. In fact it will probably give just the opposite impression. Also, there will be advertising of some sort added to your site by the web host. Again, this will probably not give the right impression to visitors, and it will to some extent divert attention from the content of your site.

Facilities

Another point to bear in mind is that free web hosting is unlikely to offer the "bells and whistles" provided by normal commercial hosting. This is only of importance if you need programming facilities, Microsoft FrontPage extensions, or similar facilities so that your web site can be equipped with clever features. This is unlikely to be an issue initially, but it might mean having to move on to a more comprehensive web hosting package at some time in the future.

One final point is that FTP access is not always possible with free web hosting. The normal way of putting a site onto the Internet is to first design and build it on a PC and then upload it to the host's server. An

FTP (file transfer protocol) program is used to upload the site to the server and to upload any changes or additions made to the site. With free web hosting it is not always possible to do things this way, and it is not the method used by some of the largest free web hosts. Instead, you have to use the software provided by the web host to produce the site. This is usually done online using software that has a wizard approach to things, making it unnecessary to have any experience with web design software. Any changes to the site are normally handled in a similar fashion. This is known as web publishing.

There is nothing intrinsically wrong with this approach to building a web site, and it is actually a very good method for beginners. You can gain some experience at web design and see your site on the Internet without spending any money or putting large amounts of time into the project. You can always move on to more sophisticated sites and building methods if you outgrow the facilities offered by the free web host. Bear in mind that the online approach to web site construction will actually cost something if you are using a pay as you go Internet connection. It could take quite a few minutes to perfect the new site.

Although some free hosts lack FTP support, they instead have their own built-in facilities for uploading pages or even complete sites. A facility of this type usually falls short of offering a true alternative to FTP access, but it might be sufficient for your needs. The option of FTP access is definitely preferable if you intend to build a complete site on your PC and then upload it to the server.

ISP hosting

At one time every Internet service provider (ISP) provided its customer with Email facilities and some free web space. The free web space is still a common feature, but it is not provided with some of the more basic connection packages. If you pay a monthly subscription fee for your Internet connection it is likely that your ISP will provide some free web space. Note though, that in most cases it is not provided automatically, and it is normally made available on request.

The amount of web space and the quality varies considerably. In general, the more you pay for your Internet connection, the greater the web space and bandwidth that will be available. I used to get five megabytes of relatively slow web space with my old dial-up connection. My new broadband connection comes complete with 50 megabytes of "professional quality" web space.

Free web space from an ISP tends to have most of the drawbacks associated with any other free web space. The web addresses tend to be long and difficult to remember, the amount of storage space and bandwidth are often limited, there may well be banner advertisements or pop-ups added to you site, commercial sites might not be allowed, and so on. In some cases it might be better to look elsewhere for free hosting.

If, on the other hand, your ISP account comes complete with plenty of fast and well featured web space with few restrictions, there might no point in going elsewhere. It will probably be necessary to do so if you really must have a short and memorable web address. Also, bear in mind that you only have the free web space while you use that particular ISP. Changing to another ISP will require the site to be moved to another server and will also involve a change of address. Even for a non-commercial site this will involve a fair amount of time and inconvenience. Changing the web address of a commercial site is something that should be avoided if at all possible.

Hired space

The monthly cost of hiring web space can be anything from a few pounds to hundreds of pounds or even more. It has the advantage that you can have any amount of storage space and bandwidth, plus any special facilities that you require, provided you are prepared to pay the monthly fee. The cheapest deals often have little more to offer than free hosting. The bandwidth and storage space will probably be relatively small, and there could still be banner advertisements or pop-ups added to you site. The range of facilities on offer is likely to be relatively limited. It is easy to get the "worst of both worlds" with a monthly fee being paid for what is still very basic hosting. Check what is on offer against the best free hosting to ensure that you are genuinely getting something extra for your money.

One advantage of practically all normal commercial hosting is that the web address will be a normal type in the usual form (name.com, name.co.uk, etc.), and not a subdomain. Note though, that there will usually be registration and other fees associated with setting up and maintaining your own web address. Make sure that the domain name is registered with you as the owner. Sometimes the web host registers the clients' domain names as its own property. This might give cost savings initially, but it tends to be more difficult and expensive if you decide to switch to another host. You may actually have no legal entitlement to the domain name with this method of registration.

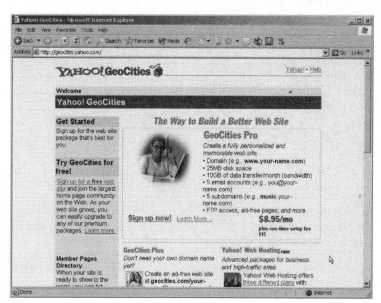

Fig.3.1 Geocities is the biggest provider of free web space

The amount of support provided varies considerably from one web host to another. Some providers offer web space at rock bottom prices, but expect the user to know how to utilize the space and sort out any minor technical difficulties. Others provide software to help you build the site and will also provide at least some technical support. One of the so-called "hold your hand" companies is a good choice for beginners. With one of these packages it should be possible to produce your site and get it running in a relatively short time.

Always check what will happen once your monthly (or whatever) bandwidth allocation is used up. In most cases visitors will be greeted with a simple screen stating that the bandwidth entitlement of the site has been used up, and that it will be back online later. A few hosts operate on the basis of a surcharge once the allotted bandwidth has been exceeded. This is a better system in that it keeps your site up and running, but there is potentially a major drawback. A few sites operating on this basis have proved to be extremely popular and have soon run up quite large bills. For a commercial site it might be worth the risk, but for non-commercial sites it is probably better to opt for the cut-off system.

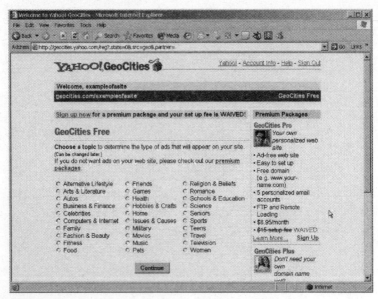

Fig.3.2 Here the preferred type of advertising is selected

Free choice

Initially it is a good idea to experiment with some free web space, provided by either your ISP or a free web hosting company. This enables valuable experience to be gained without risking any money. If the free web site suits your purposes there is no need to go any further. If it does not, it is a matter of moving on to normal commercial web hosting where you should be able to put the experience you have gained to good use. As an example of free web hosting we will use Geocities, which is now part of the Yahoo! organisation. This free web host has been selected simply because it is the biggest and best known. Geocities also hires web space incidentally. If you would like to try your own web site at Geocities, this is the address for their homepage:

http://geocities.yahoo!.com/

The Geocities homepage is shown in Figure 3.1, and the first step is to left-click the link to make your own free web page. If you are already a

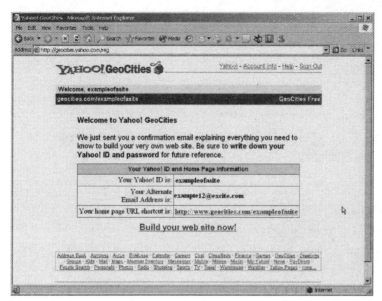

Fig.3.3 Make a note of your user ID and the password used earlier

Yahoo! member the next step is to sign in to Yahoo! in the normal way. Non-Yahoo! members must go through the registration process first. This is basically just a matter of supplying your name, address, and one or two additional details. Whichever route you take, you should end up at a page like the one shown in Figure 3.2. Here the appropriate radio button is operated to select the preferred type of advertising to appear on your site, and a wide selection is available. Note that there is no guarantee that the advertising will be in the selected category.

Having made your selection, operate the Continue button in order to move onto the next screen (Figure 3.3). This shows your user ID, and it is important to make a note of this and the password supplied during the signup process. Both of these are needed in order to make changes to your site. The address of your site is also provided, and all the free Geocities addresses take the form www.geocities.com/name, where "name" is your user ID. It is clearly a good idea to choose your ID carefully so that your site has an appropriate name. Many of the best names are already in use, so it might take a few attempts to come up with one that is suitable. You may be forced into using a longer name than you would like, due to the shorter names already being in use. It would probably

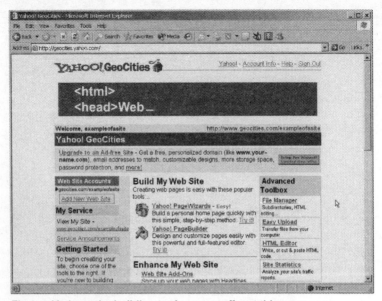

Fig.3.4 Various site building tools are on offer at this page

be advisable for existing Yahoo! users to register again in order to produce a suitable site name, rather than just using their existing ID.

Web publishing

At one time Geocities permitted web sites to be produced in the usual way and then uploaded to their server using an FTP program. This method of access is no longer available and Geocities is primarily intended for the web publishing approach to site construction. The same method is used by some other web space providers (free or otherwise), and by some ISPs that provide free web space. As pointed out previously, the general idea is that everything is handled via a web site, which in this case is obviously the Geocities site. You go into the host's web site, produce the basic pages for your site, add links, images, or whatever, and then publish the completed site on the Internet. You do not need any software for creating or uploading web pages. In most cases it is not necessary to have any knowledge of HTML, although there is often the option of using your own HTML code if preferred.

Fig.3.5 The first window when using the PageWizard

Web publishing has the obvious attractions for beginners that it is relatively simple and it avoids the need to buy any software. This method does have drawbacks though, and with some providers there is a single page limitation on sites. The wizard and templates approach to producing web pages is very simple to use, but the templates provide only a limited number of page layout options. Your site will inevitably look very similar to thousands of others. Ultimately many users outgrow the restrictions and move on to conventional web site production, but web publishing is still a good starting point.

Returning to Geocities, activating the "Build your web site now" link moves things on to the page of Figure 3.4. The links in the middle under the heading "Build my web site" are the ones that provide access to the tools that enable a site to be assembled very easily. The links to the right of this are used to access the more advanced tools such as the HTML editor. For the time being we will concentrate on the easy approach. Activating the Yahoo!! PageWizards link produces the page of Figure 3.5. Here there are a number of page layouts on offer, and it is just a matter of left-clicking the link for the page that best suits your requirements.

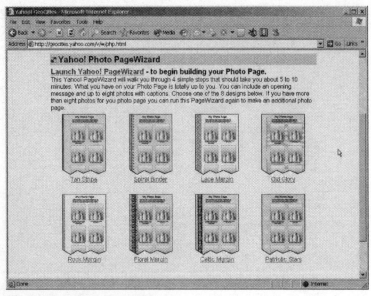

Fig.3.6 The Photo Page options

For this example I chose the Photo Page option, which produced more options (Figure 3.6). Left-clicking the link for the required page style launches the small window of Figure 3.7, and operating the Begin button moves things on to the window of Figure 3.8. This merely provides a chance to change your mind and opt for a different page style. Operating the Next button produces the window of Figure 3.9, and it is here that you start adding content to your page. A title for the page and a

Fig.3.7 Page building can now commence

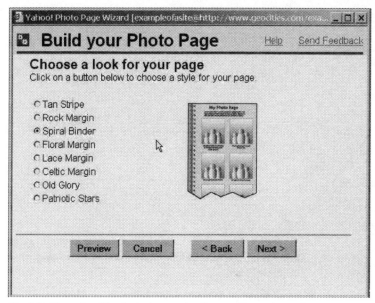

Fig.3.8 There is still a last chance to change the page style

brief introduction are added into the textboxes, and then the Next button is operated.

The first photograph is added at the next window (Figure 3.10), and the photograph will normally be stored on your PC in a web compatible format such as Jpeg. The left-hand Add Photo button is therefore operated, and at the next window (Figure 3.11) the Browse button is operated. This brings up the standard

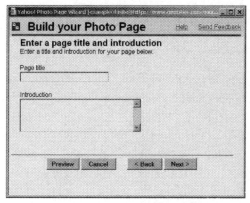

Fig.3.9 Finally, you start adding content

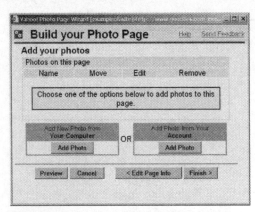

Fig.3.10 Next a photo is added to the page

Windows file browser which is used to select the correct image file. The photograph's caption and the Alt text are then added into the appropriate text boxes. The Alt text is the text that will appear if a visitor to the site places the pointer over the image. It will be displayed instead of the picture if a user has their browser set not to display images. It is not strictly necessary, but it is as well to include appropriate Alt text.

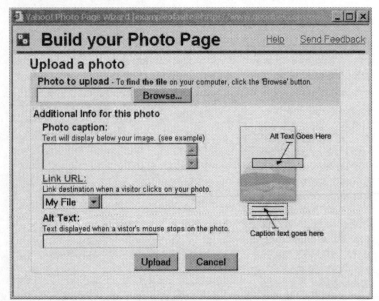

Fig.3.11 Alt text and (or) a caption can be added to the image

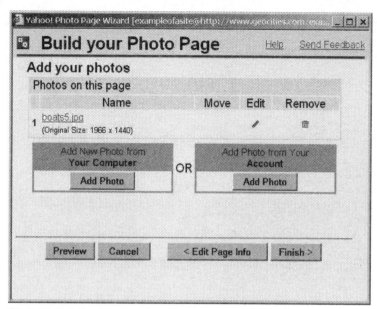

Fig.3.12 Details of the newly added image are shown here

By default the image will not be used as a link. If you would like it to act as a link to the image file, select My File from the menu and add the name of the image file in the textbox. Be sure to include the extension in the filename (e.g. boats6.jpg). The image can be used as a link to another web page by selecting Web URL using the menu and adding the correct web address in the textbox. Note that the http:// suffix is not required, and it is only the basic address that is needed (i.e. www.myotherwebsite.com). Operate the Upload button when all the necessary information has been added, and the image will be uploaded to your site. Even using a broadband connection, this can take several seconds for large image files. It could take a minute or two with a dial-up Internet connection.

With the image successfully uploaded you are taken back to the Build your Photo Page window, but it will show details of the added image in the upper section of the window (Figure 3.12). It is then a matter of repeating the process until all the images and text have been added. You then have something like Figure 3.13. From this window it is possible move images up or down in the list, remove them, or edit the text, etc., by operating the appropriate button. The page can be checked by

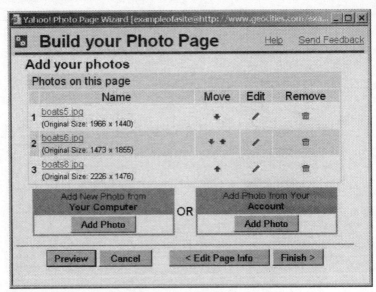

Fig.3.13 Three images have been added and are listed

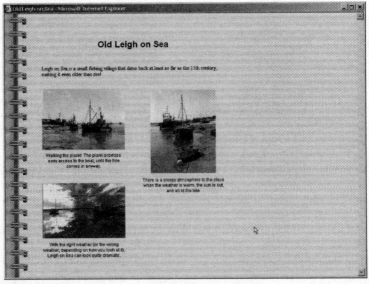

Fig.3.14 The page shown using the Preview facility

Fig.3.15 Links can be tested in the Preview facility

operating the Preview button, and the example page clearly needs another photograph to fill in the bottom right-hand corner of the page (Figure 3.14).

Preview

Links can be checked using the preview screen, and in Figure 3.15 one of the links has been tested. The photograph was used as a link to the image file, and activating the link has resulted in the photograph being displayed larger. The photograph is displayed smaller on the web page because the browser scales it to fit the allotted space. It is actually quite a high resolution image, so the browser is still scaling it down somewhat in Figure 3.15. There is little point in using image files having resolutions greater than a real world browser is ever likely to use, so where appropriate it makes sense to produce lower resolution versions of images for web use.

Having an oversize image file and a link to that file is a very simple way of enabling visitors to the site to view a larger version of an image. An on-

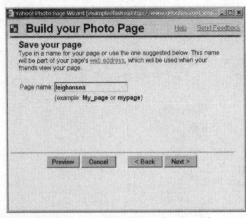

Fig.3.16 The completed page is named

screen message or the Alt text can point out to users that the image is a link to a larger version of the image. There is a drawback to this method of using the same file twice, and it is simply that the page will not be displayed properly until the image files have been downloaded. The browser requires the full image file in order to produce the scaled down version to fit the page. On the plus side, there is almost instant access to the full size images once the page has finished downloading, because the browser has already downloaded all the image files in their entirety. Anyway, if you adopt this method it is advisable to use no more image resolution than is really necessary, and to use as much compression as you dare.

When the page is completed to your satisfaction it is just a matter of operating the Finish button in the Build your Own Page window, and then in the next window (Figure 3.16) adding a name for the page in the text box. This will be part of the web address for the page, so choose something sensible. Operating the Next button completes the process, and produces the window of Figure

Fig.3.17 This window confirms that the page has been completed and shows its URL

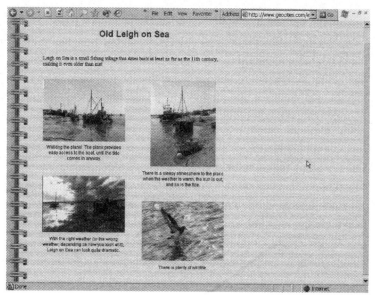

Fig.3.18 The completed page viewed via the Internet

3.17. This simply confirms that the page has been completed, and it provides the full web address for the page. At this stage the page, complete with the image files, is stored on the Geocities server, and is accessible by anyone with a web connection.

Some people mistakenly believe that the site, or parts of it such as the images, are only accessible while their computer is switched on. Of course, the point of web hosting is that it makes the site available 24 hours a day, regardless of whether your PC is switched on, and without placing any loading on your PC. Provided the server is "up and running", so is your web site. Figure 3.18 shows the page viewed via the Internet, confirming that it is indeed present and correct at the specified web address. There is no advertising on the page because the advertisements are in the form of pop-ups. The page is therefore exactly as it was designed.

This page was produced in a few minutes, even though I had no previous experience of producing a Geocities page in this way. This demonstrates just how quick and easy web publishing can be, but it is also a bit misleading. I put together the dummy page using image files left on my

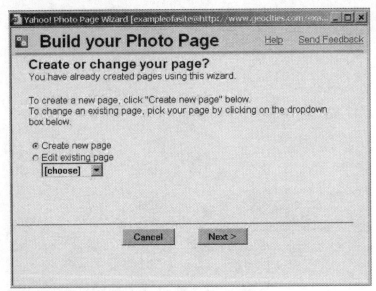

Fig.3.19 There is an option for editing your pages

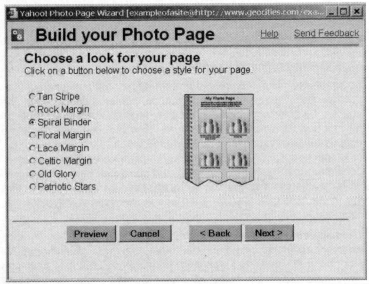

Fig.3.20 The page style can be changed here

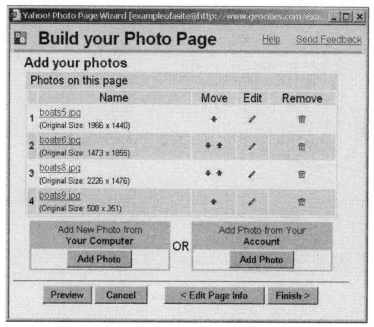

Fig.3.21 The editing facilites are the same as when initially building the page

PC after producing a previous book. It could be that all the source files for your page will already be on your computer, but in most cases it will be necessary to spend some time assembling the source material. This could easily take longer than producing the page once into the Geocities site, but it is time well spent. Repeatedly stopping work on a web page while you find or write the material for it is an inefficient way of working and is unlikely to produce good quality results.

Editing

The nature of some web sites is such that they can be left unaltered for years, but most sites need to be updated from time to time, or you might just feel like a change. To edit a page it is just a matter of signing in to Geocities again and going through the same initial steps as before. At the Build your Photo Page window there will be the choice of creating a new page or editing an existing page (Figure 3.19). Obviously the editing

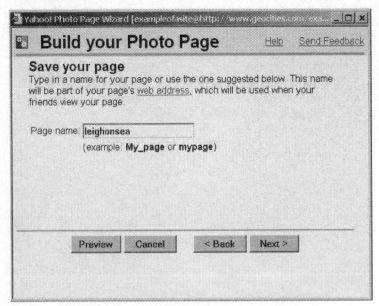

Fig.3.22 The page can be under the old name or a new one

option is chosen and the appropriate page is selected using the pop-down menu. Even if there is only one page in your site, it must still be selected using the menu.

At the next window you have the option of changing the page style (Figure 3.20), and the following window permits the text for the page to be altered. Moving on to the next window (Figure 3.21), the same editing facilities are available as when initially building the page. The page is edited in the same way as before, with the Finish button being operated once the task has been completed. If you save the page under the default name at the next window (Figure 3.22) it will overwrite and replace the previous version. The page can be saved under another name, but the original version will be left in place under the old name.

Second page

Some web publishing companies limit users to single-page sites, but with Geocities it is possible to produce multi-page sites even when using the wizard approach. So far our example site has just a single page, and it is not the home page. Using the basic address of the site under these

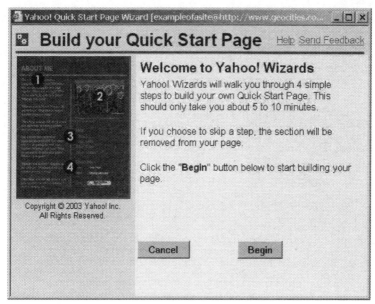

Fig.3.23 Another page can be added to the site

circumstances would normally produce the familiar error page from the browser, stating that the site was not accessible. In the case of Geocities it will probably produce a polite message stating that the site has not yet been completed. To complete the example site a home page will be added, together with a link to the existing page.

The initial process is much the same as before, but this time one of the ordinary page layouts will be chosen. This produces the introductory window of Figure 3.23, and operating the Begin

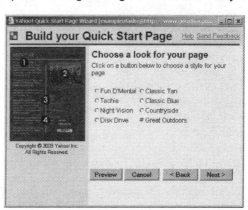

Fig.3.24 You can change the selected page layout

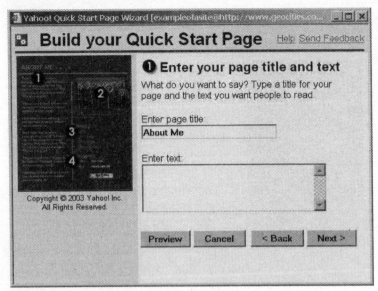

Fig.3.25 First a title and some text are added

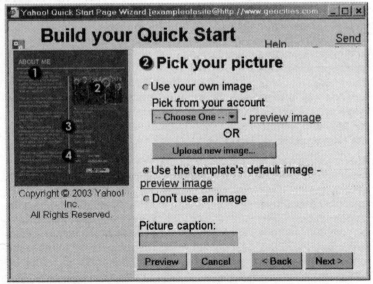

Fig.3.26 You can use the default image or add one of your own

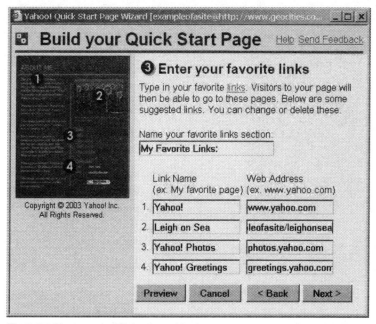

Fig.3.27 Next a set of links are added

button moves things on to the window of Figure 3.24. This just provides an opportunity to change your mind about the selected page layout. It is time to begin adding content at the next window (Figure 3.25), and the textboxes are used to add a title for the page and some text. The dummy page in the upper left-hand section of the window shows where this text will appear on the finished page. This is step one, and the material for this step is placed in the top left-hand section of the web page.

At step 2 (Figure 3.26) the image for the top right-hand section of the page is added. The template's default image can be used, as can an existing image in your site. However, in most cases it will be a matter of operating the Upload new image button and then using the standard file browser to select the required image, which must be stored somewhere on your PC. Step 3 is used to add some links below the image (Figure 3.27), and four default links are provided. Surprise, surprise, these are all for Yahoo! sites. The descriptive text and link text for each one can be edited via the textboxes, or all the text can be deleted for any links that are not required at all. In this example I have replaced one of the default

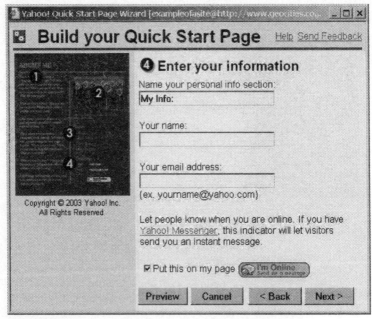

Fig.3.28 Personal information can be added, if required

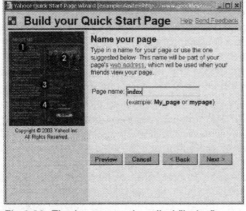

Fig.3.29 The homepage is called "index"

links with a link to the other page in the site. The fourth step (Figure 3.28) is used to add some personal information, but the textboxes can be left blank in order to omit this section of the page. In fact any section of the page can be left blank if you do not wish to include it.

Fig.3.30 This page confirms that the page has been completed

Fig.3.31 The finished page viewed in a browser via the Internet

Fig.3.32 Operating the link produces the correct page

Once the page is finished it must be named (Figure 3.29), and in this case the page is to be the homepage of the site. Therefore, it must be called "index". There is no need for visitors to the site to include the "index" section of the web address. The basic web address will reach the homepage, so in this example www.geocities.com/exampleofasite is all that has to be used as the web address. With the new page given a name the window of Figure 3.30 should appear, indicating that the page has been completed successfully. Using the basic web address in a browser did indeed reach the homepage (Figure 3.31), and activating the appropriate link produced the original page of the site (Figure 3.32). However simple or complex a site happens to be, it is essential to test it online in a browser to check that everything is displayed correctly, the links all work, the correct Alt text is produced, and so on.

From scratch

Using templates makes building web pages very quick and simple, but it is very restrictive even if a good range of templates is available. Some web publishing companies only permit this approach, but most offer

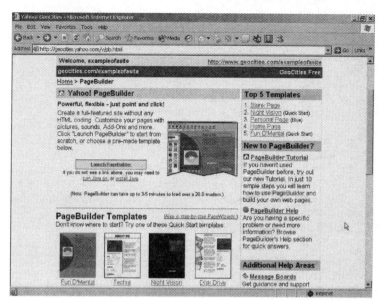

Fig.3.33 This page is used to launch the PageBuilder applet. Do not close the small window that appears, because the applet can not run without it

more flexible alternatives. In the case of Geocities their PageBuilder software can be used. This is accessed by signing in to Geocities in the usual way, and then operating the PageBuilder link on the homepage. This will bring up the web page of Figure 3.33 where the Launch PageBuilder link should be operated. A small window will be launched, and the PageBuilder applet will start to download. It is important not to close the small window even after the applet has downloaded and started to run successfully. Closing this window closes the PageBuilder applet as well.

Before too long the applet should launch and a window like the one in Figure 3.34 will appear. PageBuilder is one of the most sophisticated applets that you will encounter, and it provides what looks very much like a Windows WYSIWYG (what you see is what you get) web page construction program. This is essentially what it is, and pages can be constructed in much the same way as using a desktop publishing program. It provides a Windows-like environment complete with the familiar drop-down menus, buttons, and toolbar.

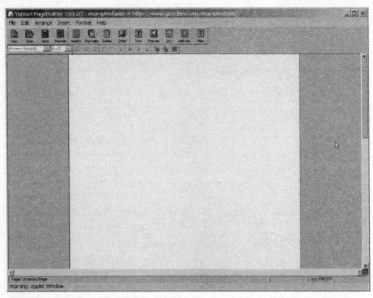

Fig.3.34 The PageBuilder applet looks much like a Windows program

Fig.3.35 This window can be used to load up to five pictures

The first task is to add something to the blank page, and for this example a picture will be added. If the picture you wish to use is not already on your site it must be uploaded first. Select Basics from the Insert menu, followed by Upload Pictures from the submenu. This produces the window of Figure 3.35 where up to five picture files can be selected. The names of the files with the full path can be typed into the textboxes, but it is easier and more reliable to use the Browse buttons and the standard file browser that these produce. Operate the Upload button when all the required files have been selected.

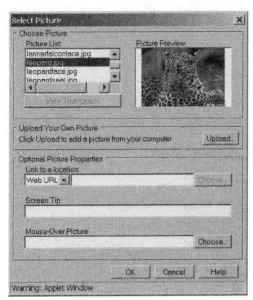

If the required picture is already on the site, or after it has been uploaded, select Basics from the Insert menu and then Pictures from the submenu. In the window that appears there is the choice of using your own files (User Files) or clipart.

Fig.3.36 A thumbnail of the selected image is displayed

Double-click on the appropriate entry in the Picture List to get a list of the available files. In the case of the Clipart option the files are stored in several folders, so it is a matter of double-clicking the entry for the appropriate folder in order to access the files. For this example the Leopard photograph in the Photos_Animals folder was selected. A thumbnail view of the selected picture is shown in the right-hand panel (Figure 3.36), so it is possible to see what an image looks like before loading it onto the page. Having found the required image, operate the OK button to go ahead and use it.

With the image on the page (Figure 3.37) it can be dragged to the desired position. A blue box and eight handles appear around the image while it is selected. The four handles in the corners can be dragged to resize the image without altering its aspect ratio. The other four handles can be used to alter the size in one direction, and obviously this method of resizing will change the image's aspect ratio. While it is useful to be able to exactly size an image to fit the available space, try to avoid anything more than minor changes to the aspect ratio. Large changes almost invariably produce some odd looking results. Avoid the temptation to substantially enlarge a small image. Doing so is likely to give some

Fig.3.37 The image can be dragged to a new position on the page

rough looking results, particularly with an image that has been subjected to a high degree of compression.

Text

Having placed an image on the page, it is time to add some text. We will start by adding a heading above the image, and the first task is to select Text from the Basics submenu. A box for the text then appears on the page, and it can be dragged into the desired position using any point within the box. There are eight handles on the box that enable it to be resized in the normal way. In order to add the text, simply left-click within the box and then type in the text in the normal way. The text will be rather small for a heading so it must be made larger. The text size menu is on the toolbar near the left end, and this provides the usual selection of seven sizes. Select all the text by dragging the text cursor through it, and then select the new size from the menu. The two largest sizes are suitable for headings. It will probably be necessary to do some resizing of the text box and (or) the image in order to get everything to fit neatly on the page.

The toolbar has many of the standard Windows text formatting tools, including popular fonts in the menu at the left end of the bar. To the right of the text size menu there are the usual buttons for left, centre, and right alignment, but there is no option for fully justified text. The next three buttons enable the text to be placed at the top, middle, or bottom of the box. A further set of three buttons give the usual bold, italic, and underline text styles. The bold style is good for headings. Remember that it is the convention that underlining is used for text that is also a link, so it is probably best not to use this text style. Underlining text that is not a link could and probably would confuse visitors to your site.

Text colour

The next button to the right enables the text colour to be altered, and it produces the small window of Figure 3.38. You can choose one of the preset colours by left-clicking on one of the swatches in the upper part of the window, or use the slider controls in the lower section to mix the required colour. Either way, the bar down the right edge of the window shows the currently selected colour. Using the next button again produces a colour selection window, but this time it is the background colour of the text box that is set. Note that you can select a single word or even a single letter and then set its colour separately from the rest of the text, but the background colour is set for the whole block of text.

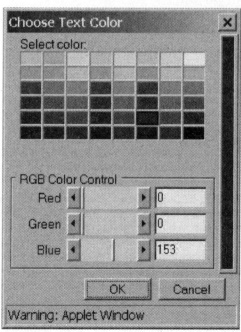

Fig.3.38 The text colour is easily changed

Good use of colour can greatly enhance web pages, but bad use of it can ruin a site. With text it pays not to get carried away with bright colours that are hard on the eye. Also, bear in mind that good contrast is needed in order to produce text that can be read easily. Here I am talking in terms of light and dark contrast rather than colour contrast. If you place some small text on the screen using contrasting colours such as red and green, with both colours at a mid tone the text will probably be difficult to read. Select a darker version of one colour and a lighter version of the other and the text will almost certainly be very much easier to read. Some monitors have difficulty accurately displaying light text on a dark background, so it is probably best to avoid this combination when using small lettering.

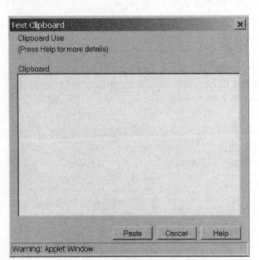

The last button brings up the Text Clipboard window (Figure 3.39). The obvious way of preparing more than a few sentences is to use a word processor and then use the normal Copy and Paste functions to transfer the text into a text box in

Fig.3.39 The Text Clipboard is used to import text from Windows applications

PageBuilder. Unfortunately, this does not work because it is not possible to directly paste text into a PageBuilder text box. Although the program looks much like an ordinary Windows type, it is in fact an applet and some of the normal Windows methods of working do not apply. The Text Clipboard provides a means of importing text that has been copied from any Windows program using the standard Copy facility.

Select the target text box, operate the Text Clipboard button, and then press the Control and V keys simultaneously to paste the text to the Text Clipboard. Then operate the Paste button to transfer the text into the text box. As far as I am aware there is no way of exporting text from the

PageBuilder applet. However, once a page has been placed on the web it is possible to load it into a browser and then use the normal Windows Copy and Paste functions to transfer the text to another application.

Rollover

Figure 3.40 shows the example page with the image and headline added, together with a small block of text to the left of the image. In the Select Picture window it was possible to add some enhancements to the image. These enhancements can be added or changed once the image is place by double-clicking on the image to bring up the Select Picture window again. The web address for a link can be entered into the top text box, and anyone left-clicking on the image will be taken to the specified page. The Screen Tip textbox is used to add Alt text. In other words, the text entered here will appear next to the pointer when it is placed over the image.

A second image can be selected using the Mouse Over Picture textbox, or the Browse button beside it. This image is selected in the same way as the first one. The Mouse Over Picture facility produces what is more commonly called a rollover. The first image is replaced by the second one when the pointer is placed over the image. A rollover can be used as a visual joke, or simply to get two images on the page when there is only room for one. It can also be useful for something like "before" and "after" images. Note that the Screen tip can be used in addition to the second rollover image. Figure 3.41 shows the dummy page with the pointer over the image, showing a newly added rollover image and some Alt text. The second image is automatically scaled to that it matches the size of the original, and the two images should therefore have a similar aspect ratio. The rollover and Alt text features do not work within PageBuilder, and must be tested using a browser.

Link text

It is often necessary to use links in text, and this is easily achieved using PageBuilder. A link can be applied to any part of a block of text, and you are not limited to applying a link to the complete block. In fact several links can be used within each block of text if necessary. In order to add a link to some text, first select the text in the usual way. Then operate the Link button, which will produce the small dialogue box of Figure 3.42. Here it is possible to enter a web address or select one of your own

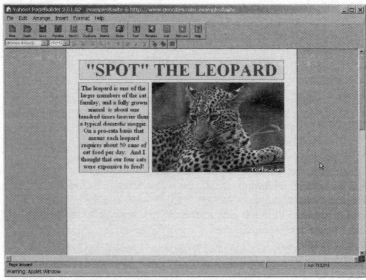

Fig.3.40 The example page, complete with image

Fig.3.41 The page with the rollover activated

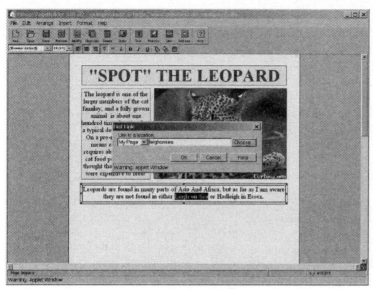

Fig.3.42 This dialogue box is used to provide the URL for the link

pages. Using the drop-down menu it is also possible to link to one of your site files or an Email address.

Figure 3.43 shows the finished page with the new block of text containing two links. The two pieces of linked text have been automatically underlined and set to a different colour to indicate that they are links. The colour of linked text can be altered just like any other text, so it is easily changed to a different colour using the method described previously.

Backgrounds

The default background is plain white, but there are plenty of alternative backgrounds available from the Backgrounds option in the Basics submenu. This option produces the Background Properties window, and operating the Set Background Color button brings up the Choose Background Color window (Figure 3.44). Here you can choose one of the preset colours from the swatches or mix your own background colour using the three slider controls. An image file from the Picture List menu

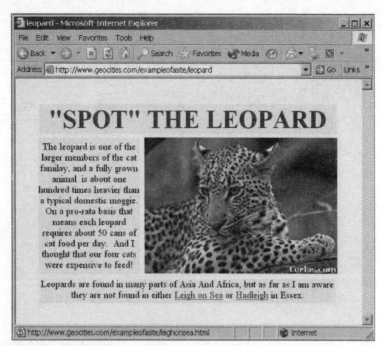

*Fig.3.43 The two links in the bottom line of text have been
automatically underlined and changed to the link colour*

is selected if something other than a plain background is required. There
are plenty of readymade backgrounds to choose from or you can use
one of your own images. In Figure 3.45 the Forest image from the
readymade backgrounds has been used.

Note that the bottom and (or) right edge of the picture will be clipped if
you use one of your own images and it is too large to fit the page. An
image that is too small will not be stretched to fit the page, but will instead
be tiled as in Figure 3.46. Results tend to look a bit scrappy if you use an
image that is quite large but is still significantly smaller than the page.
Small images, as in the example of Figure 3.46, usually give the best
effect, but avoid making the image so small that the subject becomes
barely recognisable.

If you change your mind and wish to alter the background, double-click
the square button in the bottom left-hand corner of the page to bring up
the Background Properties window again. Of course, this button only

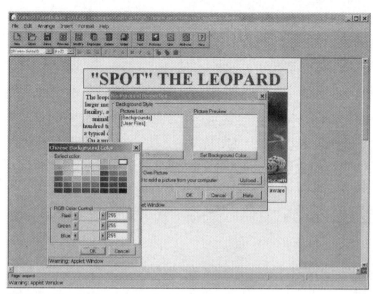

Fig.3.44 The background colour is easily changed

Fig.3.45 The dummy page with a background image added

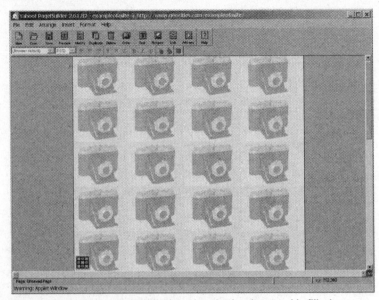

Fig.3.46 Small images are tiled so that the background is filled

appears within PageBuilder and is not included on the page when it is viewed using a browser.

Going through the backgrounds you will probably notice that they are mostly in quite pale colours, and that the photographic backgrounds are paler and have lower contrast that ordinary photographs. This is important, because the background can easily become the dominant part of the page. A good background enhances the appearance of the page without seriously distracting users from the main content. Using pastel shades is a good way of ensuring that the background does indeed stay very much in the background and does not tend to take over the page.

A useful range of backgrounds are included in the PageBuilder library, but it is quite easy to produce your own. Virtually any image that is relevant to the subject of your web site will make a suitable background if it is given suitable processing. Most graphics programs can produce gradient fills that are quite good for web page backgrounds. Figure 3.47 shows the type of thing that can be produced, although this loses something in the translation to a greyscale image. Producing your own

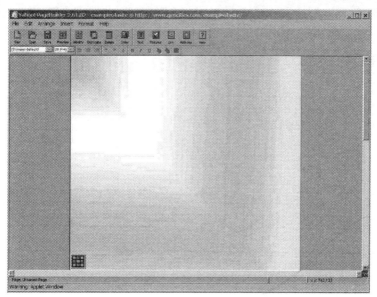

Fig.3.47 Backgrounds can be generated using a graphics program

backgrounds is covered in more detail in the next chapter, which covers the subject of web imaging in some detail.

Add-ons

The Add-ons button provides access to a wide range of objects that can be added to a page. These are also available via the menu system, and some of them, such as backgrounds, have been covered previously. Some of the objects are quite simple such as horizontal and vertical lines in various styles. Others are quite advanced and are not well suited to beginners. There are several interactive objects for example. The lines are very useful for headings and dividing pages into well defined sections. They are accessed in much the same way as backgrounds and pictures. In the example of Figure 3.48 two lines have been added to separate the large heading from the rest of the page.

It is worth taking a little time to look through the other objects and facilities on offer. Amongst the more lively offerings there are animated images that bounce around the screen. This type can be good fun in the right context, but in general it does not go down well with visitors who simply

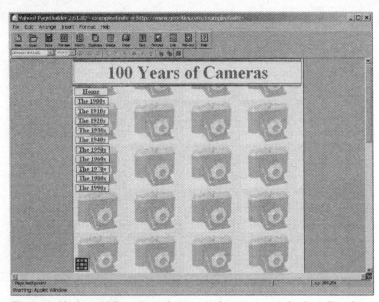

Fig.3.48 Horizontal lines have been used to separate the headline from the rest of the page

find the animated images distracting or annoying. Consequently, it is as well to use lively animations sparingly or not at all. The page effects are quite useful. The Blend effect results in one page fading out as the other "fades" in, giving a smooth transition from one page to the next. This effect gives a professional touch to a site, but it is best to use a fairly fast transition so that things are not unnecessarily slowed down.

There is free content such as news headlines and business news, but this type of thing is not really relevant to most web sites. Also, anyone requiring this type of thing will go straight to Yahoo! or another news site rather than to your pages. The Time and Date facility is useful, and it simply places the current date or time and date on the page. A range of time and date formats are available. The Counter object is also useful, and it simply indicates the number of times that a page has been accessed. If no one is visiting your pages, this will be made clear by the counter, as will the success of your site if it attracts lots of visitors. The counter can be customised to fit in well with your page layouts and colour schemes.

Menus

So far we have only considered some example pages and the ways that they can be produced using the Geocities version of web publishing. A real site is not a selection of random pages, but a set of pages having a common theme. There must be links to enable users to move easily from one page to another. With large sites it is difficult to provide easy links from each page to every other page due to the large number of links that would be required on each page. It generally requires several pop-up menus to achieve this sort of thing. It is much easier with a site that has only a few pages, since it requires only one simple menu per page. In most cases the same menu is used on each page, which makes it easy for users to move from page to page.

The simplest way of making a menu is to use a block of text with the appropriate link applied to each piece of text within the block. An alternative is to use separate blocks of text to give a simple button style menu, and this method has been used in the dummy menu on the page in Figure 3.48. It is advisable to start by putting in the longest piece of text, and the use the Copy and Paste facilities to produce the required number of menu buttons. This ensures uniformity of size. With the text in each button edited to the correct word or words, the link for each piece of text is added.

It can be difficult to get the buttons lined up and spaced neatly, but PageBuilder has a

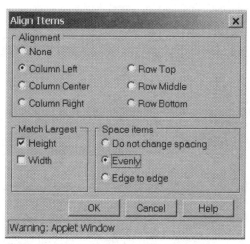

Fig.3.49 The Align Items control panel

solution to the problem in the form of the Align function in the Arrange menu. All the buttons must be selected before invoking this command, and there should be nothing else selected. Objects are selected using the normal Windows methods. One way of making multiple selections

is to hold down the Control key and then left-click on each item to be included in the selection. Where the objects are grouped together it is possible to select them by dragging a box around the objects, being careful to include nothing else within the box.

Fig.3.50 The "before" version of the buttons

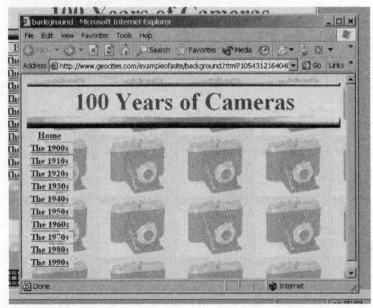

Fig.3.51 The "after" version, with the buttons correctly aligned

Aligning objects

The Align Items control panel of Figure 3.49 appears when the Align function is used. In this case a column of objects on the left edge of the page is being aligned, so the Column Left alignment option is used. The Match Largest option is irrelevant in this case, since all the buttons are the same size. Even spacing as well as alignment is required, so the Evenly option is selected. On operating the OK button the selected objects are aligned and spaced correctly, as demonstrated by the "before" and "after" views of Figures 3.50 and 3.51 respectively.

It is easy to make changes to pages using PageBuilder. The File menu has what appears to be the usual Open Page, Save, and Save As options. However, bear in mind that these do not open and save pages on the hard disc of your PC. These functions operate directly on the pages of your site on the Geocities server. Therefore, in order to edit a page it is merely necessary to open it, make the changes, and then save it again. Use the New Page option to start a fresh page, and add it to your site using the Save or Save As option once it is completed.

When using the same basic page layout for all or several pages in a site the usual approach is to start by making a template page that has the required background, heading, menus, links, and so on. Next this page is saved under an appropriate name such as "template" or "outline". To make a page for the site it is then just a matter of opening this page, making any necessary changes, adding the content, and saving it under a new name. This avoids having to add the same basic objects each time a new page is started, and it also gives uniformity of style from one page to the next.

It is not possible here to go into all the facilities of PageBuilder. Fortunately, some of the more basic facilities are sufficient to build some good web pages and combine them into an effective web site. More advanced features can be added later on as more experience is gained. Building web sites using PageBuilder is about as easy as it gets, so there is little point in bothering with the template approach unless you require something more than a few very simple web pages.

Other tools

Geocities does not force users into using the web publishing approach to site construction and maintenance, and it is possible to use a more conventional approach using facilities of the Advanced Toolbox on the

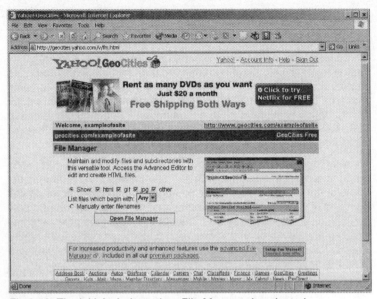

Fig.3.52 The initial window when File Manager is selected

Geocities homepage. The File Manager does what you would expect it to. Selecting this option produces the initial page of Figure 3.52, where you can apply filters so that only certain types of file are displayed. The same filter options are available from the File Manager program itself, in the lower section of the main screen.

Launching File Manager produces a window like the one in Figure 3.53, where all the files in the site will be listed. It is files rather than pages that are listed, so any images files will be listed, together with the page files. The latter are those having an htm or html extension to the basic filenames. Any file can be viewed by left-clicking the appropriate View link, and some statistics are available for the web pages. These are accessed via the Stats links, and the page that appears provides some basic statistics such as the number of times the page was visited and the web browser program used by the majority of users. If you wish to know the number of times that each page has been visited but you would prefer this information not to be made available to others, use this counter facility instead of having a counter on each web page.

A file can be selected using its checkbox, and it is then possible to edit, copy, rename, or delete it by operating the appropriate button. Editing a

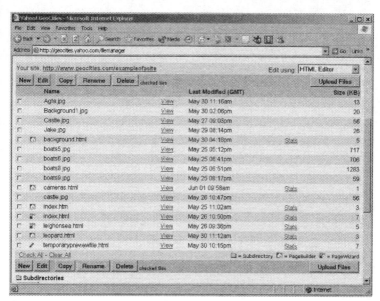

Fig.3.53 File Manager lists all the files in the site

page produces a simple HTML editor (Figure 3.54), together with a warning message if the page was produced using PageBuilder. Any changes made to the HTML code will be applied to the page correctly, but they will be lost again if the page is subsequently edited with PageBuilder. In fact most web page creation programs have "strings attached", and you can not freely mix your own HTML code with the automatically generated code. In general it is better to use either a web page creation program or your own code, and not a mixture of the two. Note that the Edit facility is only applicable to HTML files. Image files must be edited prior to uploading. If additional editing is needed, edit the image file stored on you computer, delete the image file on your site, and then upload the edited image to replace the deleted one.

The Upload Files button brings up PageBuilder's version of a file browser, so that the required files can be selected easily and then uploaded to your site. This is potentially very useful, since it makes it possible to create simple sites using normal web creation software and then upload the site via File Manager. Remember that ordinary FTP access is not possible with Geocities, and it is also unavailable with some other web space providers. Without an upload facility of this type it is otherwise

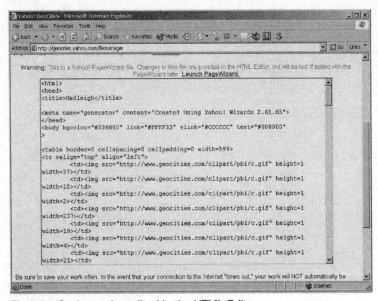

Fig.3.54 Code can be edited in the HTML Editor

impossible to create and upload sites using ordinary web creation programs.

Note that the upload facility is also available direct from the Easy Upload link on the Geocities homepage. The HTML Editor link on the homepage provides access to essentially the same facility that is used for editing existing pages, but it is preloaded with the outline code for a blank page (Figure 3.55). A Table Maker facility is available (Figure 3.56), but this is about the only assistance on offer. Unless you really know what you are doing it is best to forget about using this method. The Site Statistics option on the Geocities homepage simply provides direct access to site statistics, such as the number of times each page has been viewed.

Photo albums

The Geocities version of web publishing includes a template for producing a page of photographs, and this is fine if you wish to make a few photographs available to everyone via the Internet. There is a better way of doing things though, if you wish to share a larger number of

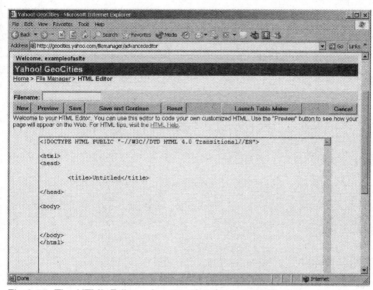

Fig.3.55 The HTML Editor when starting from scratch

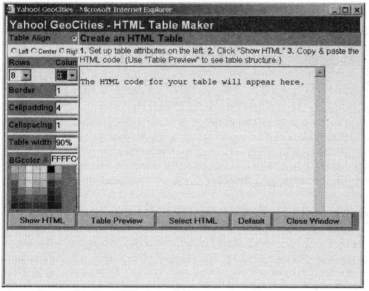

Fig.3.56 The editor includes a table generator facility

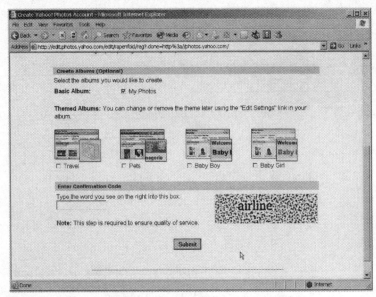

Fig.3.57 Templates for various type of album are available

photographs and (or) restrict access so that only your family and friends can view the photographs. This better method is an online photo album. Most types of free web space have been in decline in recent years, but there seems to be an ever increasing number of companies offering online photo album facilities. Any Internet search engine should soon produce a list of sites that provide this facility.

Yahoo! has a photo album facility that offers a very reasonable limit of 90 photographs and 30 megabytes. In order to make use of the Yahoo! photo album facility it is necessary to register as a Yahoo! member if you are not already a Yahoo! or Geocities member. The online album facility can be accessed via the Photos link in the Organise section of the www.yahoo.com homepage. During the initial stages of setting up the album you may be offered the choice of producing special types of album (Figure 3.57), but here we will produce the standard type.

You will probably have to type the "hidden" word into the textbox in order to continue with the process. This is rapidly becoming a standard feature when obtaining any form of free web space. It is designed to stop automated systems from setting up numerous false accounts for use by

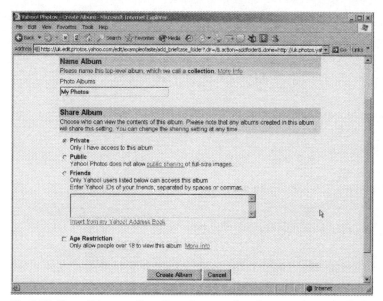

Fig.3.58 *From this page the album is named and access is controlled*

those looking for free storage space for their porno sites, pirated software, etc. You should be able to decipher the word quite easily, but it is very difficult for automated systems to do so.

The first task when you start creating the album is to name the album and choose the amount of access there will be to the site (Figure 3.58). In the case of the Yahoo! album facility you can have the site for you own use only, for use by the listed Yahoo! members, or there can be general access. With general access the photographs might not be available at full resolution. This is presumably done to deter illegitimate use of the photo album facility. There is also a facility to block those under 18 years of age from viewing the album.

Adding photographs

At the next page your new album is displayed, but obviously it is empty at this stage (Figure 3.59). In order to start adding photographs it is merely necessary to left-click the Start Adding Photographs link, which will bring up the page shown in Figure 3.60. Here the filenames of the

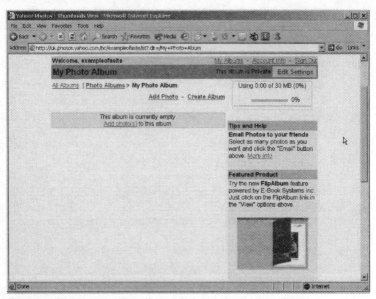

Fig.3.59 At this stage the album obviously lacks any pictures

photographs, complete with the full path, can be added into the textboxes. Alternatively, operate the Browse button and use the file browser to select each image file. The photographs should be in a standard web format, and Jpeg is probably the best option. Scroll down to the bottom of the page and operate the Upload button to go ahead and upload the images, or operate the Cancel button if you wish to abort the operation.

If all goes well a confirmation screen like the one shown in Figure 3.61 will appear. This lists the photographs that have been successfully uploaded. By operating the appropriate link it is possible to add more photographs to the album or return to the album page. Figure 3.62 shows the album page with some more pictures added. In order to view one of the pictures larger it is merely necessary to left-click on its thumbnail view on the album page (Figure 3.63). With high resolution pictures this will not produce a full-size view of the image.

A low resolution thumbnail image is automatically generated when each photograph is uploaded, and so is a medium resolution version. It is the medium resolution image that is displayed when the thumbnail version is left-clicked. This has a much smaller image file that will download much more quickly than the full-size version. The image can be viewed

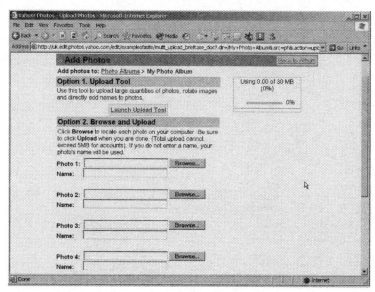

Fig.3.60 This page is used to select and upload the photographs

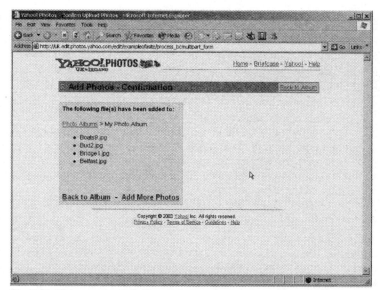

Fig.3.61 This screen lists the photographs that have been uploaded

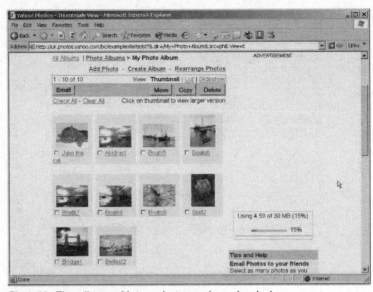

Fig.3.62 The album with ten photographs uploaded

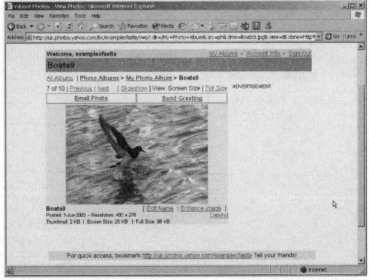

Fig.3.63 Larger versions of the pictures can be viewed

Fig.3.64 The highest resolution images may not fit the screen, but all the picture can be accessed using the scrollbars

at maximum resolution by left-clicking the Full Size link that is above and to the right of the medium resolution version. Note though, that a high resolution image will be too large to fit the screen even if a fairly high screen resolution is used (Figure 3.64). The entire image is still accessible, but only with the aid of the scrollbars. Of course, there will only be a higher resolution version if the resolution of the original image was high enough to make this possible.

Image editing

There are various facilities available from the album page and when an individual image is viewed. The Rename facility enables the name of the image to be changed, but it also permits a short description to be added (Figures 3.65 and 3.66). The Enhance Image facility produces a window that provides some basic image editing facilities (Figure 3.67). It is better to undertake this type of thing using image editing software prior to uploading images, but this method is worth a try if you do not have access to suitable software.

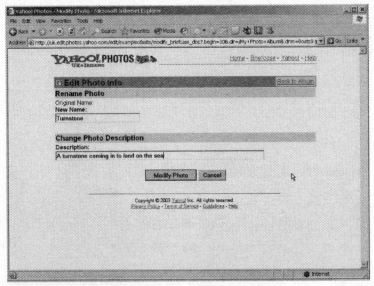

Fig.3.65 A short description can be added to a picture

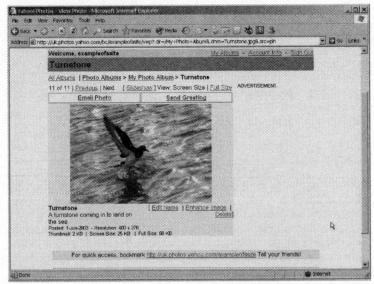

Fig.3.66 One of the pictures with a description added

Fig.3.67 Some basic image editing facilities are available

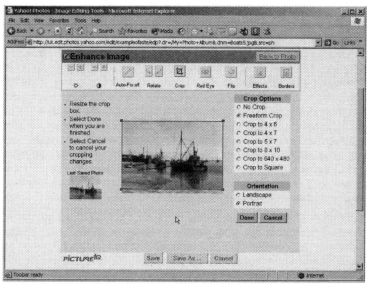

Fig.3.68 A useful image cropping facility is available

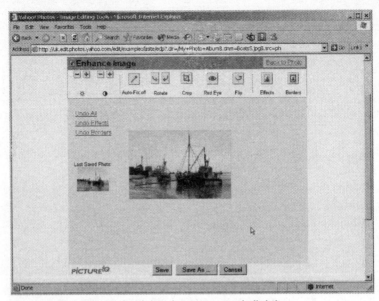

Fig.3.69 The image after it has been cropped slightly

The image cropping facility is potentially useful, and selecting this option produces the window of Figure 3.68. A box appears around the image and its size can be adjusted via the handle at each corner. The box can be dragged to a new position by "grabbing" anywhere within its boundary. The radio buttons to the right of the image enable the cropping box to be constrained to one of several aspect ratios. These aspect ratios match those of popular print sizes, and are useful if you intend to make use of online printing services. Simply adjust the size and position of the box to make it encompass only the parts of the image you wish to retain, and then operate the Done button. Of course, it might be necessary to compromise slightly on the composition of the cropped image if the aspect ratio of the cropping box is fixed. Figure 3.69 shows a cropped version of the fishing boat photograph.

The Effects button provides access to a limited but useful range of filter effects (Figure 3.70). When an effect is selected it is applied to the image in the main window, so it is possible to quickly run through the effects to see what each one looks like when applied to the image. Activate the Close Window link when the required effect has been selected. Operate

Fig.3.70 A small but useful range of filter effects is available

the No Effect link first if you wish to exit the Effects window without adding any filtering.

Operate the Save or Save As button in order to save the filtered image and add it to the album. The page of Figure 3.71 appears when the Save option is used. This warns you that the Save function will overwrite the original image, and it provides an opportunity to save a copy of the photograph. In other words, the original image can be retained and the filtered version is saved under another name. I opted for the Save Copy facility, and in the album page (Figure 3.72) the filtered image has been added to the album, with the original being retained.

It is worth experimenting with the Effects facility as it is possible to produce some interesting effects. The filtering of Figure 3.71 has produced a charcoal drawing effect. The Pastel filter also produces an artistic effect, effectively turning a photograph into a pastel sketch (Figure 3.73). The Neon filter produces a more extreme glowing edge effect (Figure 3.74). It is also possible to produce extreme filtering by using two or three types of filtering in succession.

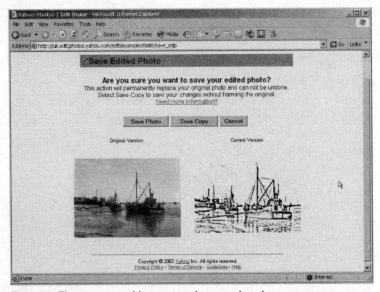

Fig.3.71 *The processed image can be saved under a new name*

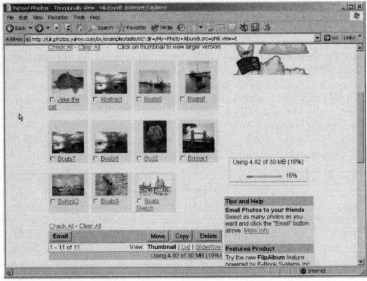

Fig.3.72 *The cropped and filtered image added to the album*

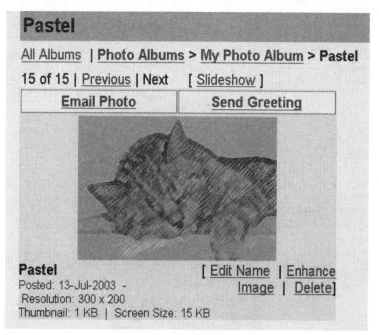

Fig.3.73 Pastel filtering has been used with this image

Finally

Web publishing is probably not the route to take if you require a large and complex site, but it is certainly worth considering where something reasonably straightforward is required. Although it is regarded by many as the "poor relation" of "proper" web site construction, the better web publishing systems are now extremely good. There is no reason for a site produced using one of these systems to be inferior to one produced using conventional web site construction software. Moreover, producing a site in this way is more or less guaranteed to be easier than conventional methods.

There are a couple of drawbacks to consider, and one is simply that there are relatively few providers of web publishing facilities. A good range of providers is still available though, and it should be possible to find something that suits most needs. Perhaps of more importance to

GlowEffect---1

Email Photo	Send Greeting

GlowEffect---1   [Edit Name | Enhance Image |
Posted: 13-Jul-2003 - Resolution: 267 x   Delete]
400
Thumbnail: 2 KB | Screen Size: 31 KB | Full Size: 689 KB

Fig.3.74 The Neon filtering produces a more extreme effect, but it can work quite well with an image that has strong outlines

many, web publishing requires the user to be online while the site is created, and when any subsequent changes are made to the site. This is not a problem for those having broadband or some other form of non-metered Internet access, but it could otherwise be relatively expensive.

Points to remember

Web publishing avoids the need for knowledge of HTML coding, or software to create and upload your web site. Instead, the site is created online using the page creation facilities provided by the web host. Web publishing is mainly associated with free web hosting, but some hired web space has the option of using this method of site construction.

Some web publishing hosts limit the user to one page per site. Unless you really need just a single page site, seek out a provider that provides the facilities for building sites that have multiple pages.

The simplest approach to web publishing is to use a template for each page. The most suitable layout is selected from those on offer, and the content is then added to each section of the page. It is possible to produce almost instant web pages using this system, but it has some major drawbacks. The main one is that your web site has to be "moulded" to suit the available templates, which may or may not be well suited to your requirements.

Some web publishing sites have quite sophisticated applets that enable pages to be designed to suit your exact requirements. The facilities are very much like those of simple desktop publishing programs. The finished web pages should look virtually identical to the layouts produced on the WYSIWYG display used when designing them.

There are often a lot of add-ons available. Some of these, such as counters, are simple to use and very useful. Others are simple to use but of limited practical value. Avoid clever tricks that will simply irritate users and keep them away from your site. Some of the add-ons are quite sophisticated, but are beyond the scope of beginners. It is useful to have these facilities available in case you wish to move on to this type of thing later.

If you simply need to produce an online photo album there are web publishing sites specifically for this type of thing. In fact there seems to be an ever growing number of album sites. In most cases the albums can be for your own viewing only, for viewing by selected friends and members of your family, or by the general public.

Some album sites have additional facilities, such as simple photo-editing capabilities (cropping, filtering, red-eye reduction, etc.). These are useful if you do not have any image editing software, but it is worth obtaining a good but inexpensive photo-editing program if you produce more than the occasional digital image.

Web graphics

Pixels

In order to use an image in a web site it must be in digital form, which means either taking the picture using a digital camera or scanning a photograph. Actually, for the best possible quality from the scanning method it is best to scan the negative or transparency using a film scanner, but for web use scanning a photographic print should produce more than adequate quality. Provided the print is of reasonable quality, even quite a small print will produce adequate quality for most web use. Film scanners are relatively expensive, and are considerably over specified for web applications. In fact the cheapest of flatbed scanners should produce adequate quality for the vast majority of web applications. Scans at very high resolutions are pointless if the resolution of the scanned image has to be massively reduced in order to make it fit a web page.

A digital image of the type produced by scanners and digital cameras is comprised of numerous dots, or pixels as they are termed. Normally the individual pixels are too small to be seen, but they can be seen quite clearly in a magnified view of a digital image. Figure 4.1 shows a digital image and Figure 4.2 shows a highly zoomed view of some of the mud in the foreground of the picture. Many of the individual pixels can be seen in the highly zoomed version. Highly magnified areas of digital images are not usually recognisable, but everything looks fine with the pixels at such a small size that they blend to form a proper image. Because the pixels have to be very small in order to blend into a proper image, it requires large numbers of them in order to produce an image of reasonable size. In fact it takes many thousands of pixels to produce even a small image.

The maximum number of pixels per image is something that is usually at or near the top in digital camera specifications, and it is often alluded to in the names of the cameras. The situation is similar with scanners, where the name often alludes to the maximum resolution in dots per inch. It is normally a case of the more pixels the better, but resolution is

Fig.4.1 In a normal view the individual pixels are not discernible

not usually an issue with web images. You may wish to include high resolution images on your site, but most images used on the web have quite low resolutions. Something like 350 by 250 pixels is quite typical, and many web images are smaller than that. The number of pixels per image is quite large, and would be some 87,500 for a 350 by 250 pixel image. This is still quite low by the standards of normal digital imaging, where the number of pixels is often into the millions.

Any digital camera or flatbed scanner should be able to produce images having adequate resolution for use on web pages. In most cases the initial resolution of the image will be far too high and it will have to be reduced. Of course, when buying a scanner or digital camera it might be better to pay extra for one having a higher specification than that required for producing web images. The equipment will then be good enough for other purposes, such as making good quality prints. If you really need to produce nothing more than low resolution web images, practically any digital camera or flatbed scanner will probably suffice. Bear in mind though, that very wide angle shots, extreme close-ups, and other technically advanced shots will probably require a sophisticated camera. You might obtain adequate resolution from a cheapie camera, but it could be inadequate in other respects.

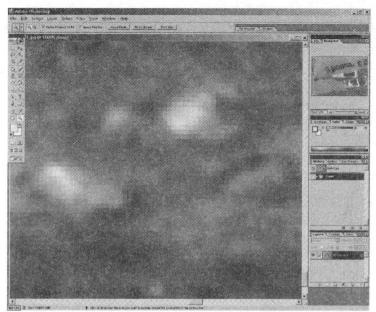

Fig.4.2 This zoomed view shows the individual pixels

Detail

It is important to realise that using low resolution images severely limits the amount of details that can be included in a picture. Low resolution images, whether or not they are for use on the Internet, generally work best with simple compositions that have just one significant item of subject matter. For example, with pictures of people a low resolution image will usually work well if the picture is of just one person. A group shot will be recognisable as a group of people, but it is unlikely that any individuals in the shot would be recognisable. A tightly cropped portrait is likely to be more recognisable than a full-length shot having the same number of pixels.

Figures 4.3 and 4.4 help to illustrate the problems encountered when using low resolution images. Figure 4.3 is a picture of a bird at a resolution of about 370 by 300 pixels. This size is small enough to give fast download times in Internet applications, but it is also high enough to show a reasonable amount of detail on a tightly cropped picture such as this. An ornithologist would probably have no difficulty in identifying the bird as a turnstone. Suppose that a picture of a group of birds was used

Fig.4.3 The original image

instead of a picture of a single bird, with the number of pixels per bird being reduced by a factor of ten in each direction. This would reduce each bird to something like Figure 4.4, which has a complete lack of detail and is barely recognisable as any sort of bird.

Of course, on a web page the pixels would not be large, and the smaller size helps to make them merge together into a more obvious representation of a bird. Figure 4.5 shows the original image with the reduced version added near the top right-hand corner. This time the reduced version has not been scaled up, and it looks more plausible this way. In fact it looks reasonably good, but the shape is quite distinctive and easily recognisable. The human brain is very good at making the most of a limited amount of visual detail, especially with something familiar such as a bird. Results would be less impressive with many types of subject matter. It also pays to bear in mind that the physical size of the whole image could be quite small as displayed by many computers, and in such cases a small part of the image would be minute.

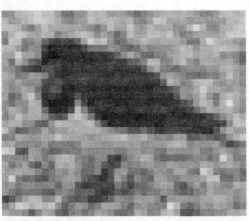

Fig.4.4 With lower resolution the bird is barely recognisable

With this type of thing it is necessary to take each case on its own merits. If the purpose of a photograph is to show a certain species of bird flocking together in large numbers, then it must show a reasonable number of birds in order to properly make the point. However, the individual birds still need to recognisable as such. Where necessary, use a slightly higher resolution picture than normal. It is better to have a slightly longer download time and a page that works, than one that downloads quickly but has unrecognisable images.

If a detailed image of an individual bird was needed as well, this could be included as a separate image or as an inset on the main image. A giant-size picture of a flock of birds would not be

Fig.4.5 The lower resolution image inset (top right) on the original image

a good way of handling things. The image would take forever to download and in all probability there would still be no really good representation of a single bird. In general, two or three small images will make the point better than one huge picture, and the total download time for the small images is likely to be much less.

Rollovers are ideal for a situation where a group shot and a close-up of an individual are needed. Have the group shot as the normal picture and the close-up as the rollover image. It works well the other way round with the close-up as the main image, but most people prefer to have the group shot normally on screen with the rollover effectively giving a zoomed view. Remember to include a short onscreen instruction explaining that placing the pointer over the image will give a close-up shot. There is otherwise no guarantee of visitors finding the rollover image.

Why process?

On the face of it, there is no need to undertake any processing with images for web use. If an image is suitable for printing, desktop publishing, or whatever, it should also be suitable for use on a web site. In practice matters are not as simple as that, and the requirements for Internet use are slightly different to those for most other applications. Admittedly, an image needs to be technically good whether it will be published on the Internet, printed, or used in any other way. If an image has the correct contrast, colour balance, etc., for printing, then it should also have the correct settings for web use.

However, there is more to using images on the web than getting the contrast, brightness and colour settings correct. As already pointed out, file size is of great importance for web images, where fast download times are important. Large files produce long download times and are best avoided. File size is not really a consideration in most other applications. Actually, producing images for the Internet is the opposite of most other applications in this respect. Large image files are generally considered desirable since they give higher quality results. It follows from this that by reducing the size of an image file for web use the image quality will be compromised.

It is true that processing an image file for web use will usually result in some loss of quality, but it will not necessarily produce a significant loss of quality. The first point to understand is that modern sources of digital images tend to produce a certain amount of quality "overkill" for web use. A normal size photographic print scanned at 300 dots per inch will produce an image having around 1800 by 1200 pixels. A "jumbo" size print scanned at 600 dots per inch would produce an image having around 5400 by 3600 pixels. The resolutions of modern digital cameras vary considerably, but in general the maximum image size is about 1024 by 768 pixels or larger. Many cameras produce images having three or four times as many pixels as this.

An average computer screen has a horizontal screen resolution of around 800 to 1280 pixels. A lesser number of pixels will usually be available for displaying images. The browser will normally reduce an image to fit the screen if it is too large to fit at its natural resolution. The alternative is for scrollbars to appear so that the user can pan around the image, which is never displayed in its entirety. This second method is not popular with users, who are more likely to move on to another page than start scrolling around outsize images. Therefore, in most cases it is pointless putting large images onto web sites. Users will either view them at lower resolutions or simply not look at them at all. Even if you do not bother with any other image processing, it is important to a least resize large images so that they will comfortably fit onto web pages.

Compression

There are two aspects to keeping the sizes of image files to a minimum. One is simply to use the lowest acceptable resolution, and the other is to apply compression to the image. Compression is built in to many popular image file formats, but it is by no means a feature of them all. The image file format normally used for the Internet is Jpeg (also known as Jpg). This supports various types of compression and the amount of compression can be varied. Any web browser should be able to properly display a Jpeg image regardless of the amount and type of compression used.

Whether called Jpeg or Jpg, the name of this format is pronounced jay-peg. It is now the most common format used for bitmaps. A bitmap is simply an image that is made up of pixels, and practically all digital photographs are in this form. Jpeg is not only used for web images, but it is excellent in this role because of its ability to reduce complex images to quite small amounts of data. The modest file size is achieved using large amounts of compression, although lesser amounts of compression can be used if high quality is of prime importance. With some image editing programs you can use varying degrees of compression and up to three different types, but not all are this accommodating.

A great deal of development has gone into compression techniques for image files. Unfortunately, it is still the case that small file sizes obtained using high degrees of compression are obtained at the expense of reduced picture quality. In Internet applications it is clearly helpful to have small files in order to keep download times to a minimum. On the other hand, there is no point in having an image that downloads very quickly if no one can see what it is meant to be! The borderline between acceptable and unacceptable quality is a subjective matter, and can only be determined using the "suck it and see" approach.

Figure 4.6 shows a photograph that has been saved in Jpeg format using minimal compression, and Figure 4.7 shows the same photograph with maximum compression. These produce file sizes of about 900k and 100k respectively, and there is surprisingly little difference between them. However, with a colour image any artefacts added by the compression tend to be more noticeable, so this monochrome image is perhaps

Fig.4.6 At about 900k this Jpeg image has minimal compression

overstating the case for using large amounts of compression. However, it does demonstrate the fact that large amounts of compression do not necessarily produce very poor quality. Compression works well with some types of subject matter but is less impressive with others.

It is often images that have detailed and plain areas in close proximity that show the most obvious signs of problems when large amounts of compression are used. Figure 4.8 shows two icons on the Windows Desktop of my PC, and this image has been stored using minimal Jpeg compression. The image file is substantially smaller than an equivalent bitmap having no compression, but there are no obvious signs of compression having been used. Figure 4.9 shows the same image, but stored using as much compression as possible. The two icons are

Fig.4.7 Even compressed to about 100k the quality is quite good

perhaps slightly less distinct in this version, but the most noticeable problem is all the rubbish that has been added around the icons and the lettering in what should be plain areas of the image.

There are no "hard and fast" rules about the maximum amount

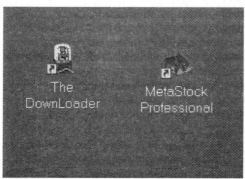

Fig.4.8 The "clean" image

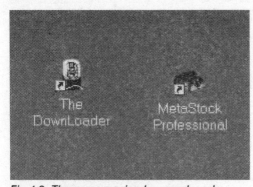

*Fig.4.9 The compression has produced
noticeable artefacts*

of compression that can be used. Some images work well with compression while with others even modest amounts of compression produce noticeable artefacts. In the end it is a subjective matter, and the maximum usable compression depends on the loss of detail and (or) added artefacts you are prepared to tolerate. One thing is not debatable though. In order to get image files down to reasonable sizes it is definitely necessary to use compression.

Pick of the crop

Having scanned your image or taken a suitable photograph, how do you go about preparing it for use on a web page? Some sort of image editing software is needed, and something suitable might have been supplied with your camera or scanner. If not, there are plenty of good image editing programs available at reasonable prices. The exact way in which photo-editing tasks are handled varies slightly from one program to another. The examples provided here therefore have to be representative of the general way in which these tasks are handled. Things will probably be slightly different with the software you use, but not radically different.

Some image editing programs use a wizard approach to processing images, or offer this as an option. Others offer what is really a conventional menu approach to things, but with the menus arranged and presented in a way that makes the program easier for beginners to use. Ulead Photo Express 3.0 SE is typical of the bundled software supplied with low-cost scanners and cameras, and it uses the simplified menu approach (Figure 4.10).

You might be entirely happy with the composition of an image, but in most cases some cropping will improve the picture. With low resolution images it is generally better not to have too much extraneous material

Fig.4.10 Photo Express 3.0 SE uses a simplified menu approach

around the main subject. This would simply serve to make what is already a fairly small image appear to be even smaller. The image is unlikely to look right if it is cropped so tightly that the main subject actually touches the edges, but results could be best with the cropping nearly as tight at that. It is necessary to use your judgement when cropping an image.

In Photo Express an image is cropped by activating the Selection menu and then operating the Shape button. Rectangular, square, circular, and elliptical shapes are available when cropping, but note that the image will still be rectangular if circular or elliptical cropping is used. The popular file formats only support rectangular images, so when a different shape is used there is a blank area outside the main image to fill out the rectangle. In this case a rectangle will suffice as the cropping shape. The required rectangle is simply dragged onto the image (Figure 4.11), and then the button marked "Crop with current selection" is operated. This produces the cropped version of the image (Figure 4.12).

A slightly different approach is used in the upmarket Photoshop 7 image editor, and lower cost version, Photoshop Elements 2. The latter, or its predecessor, are often bundled with mid-range to upmarket digital

Fig.4.11 A rectangle is dragged onto the screen

cameras and scanners. Both versions of the program have a Toolbox down the left edge of the screen (Figure 4.13), and simple rectangular cropping is achieved by selecting the Crop tool. This is again used to drag a rectangle onto the screen, and the area outside the rectangle is shown much darker than normal. This makes it easy to see what the cropped version of the picture will look like. The rectangle can be repositioned by dragging it around the screen, and it can be resized by dragging the corners and edges. When the rectangle is exactly as required the Return key is operated and the image is cropped (Figure 4.14).

Photoshop offers alternative ways of cropping an image, and one of these is to use the Marquee tool. This can be used to drag a rectangle onto the screen in the usual way, but it has an alternative mode where the size of the rectangle can be specified in pixels. If you needed to crop the image at (say) 500 by 400 pixels, these dimensions would be entered into the Height and Width textboxes, and a rectangle of this size would then appear on the screen. The rectangle would then be dragged into position so that the required part of the image was selected, and then the Return key would be operated to go ahead and crop the image.

Fig.4.12 The cropped version of the image

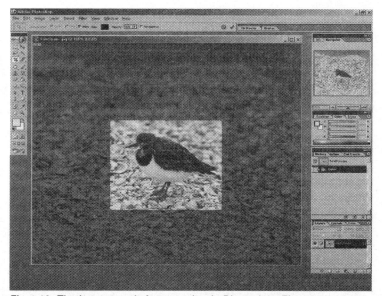

Fig.4.13 The image ready for cropping in Photoshop Elements

Fig.4.14 A zoomed view of the cropped image

Fig.4.15 Various cropping masks are available in Photo Express 3.0

Feathering

Most image editing programs can provide something beyond basic cropping. Photo Express has a more complex mode that enables various shapes to be used when cropping (Figure 4.15). In this example an ellipse has been chosen, but there are more complex shapes available such as clover, flower, and heart shapes. The selected shape is dragged to the required size and into

Fig.4.16 The cropped image using feathering

position. The image can simply be cropped with "hard" edges, but an effect known as feathering is often utilized when something other than simple rectangular cropping is used. The Soft Edge options in Photo Express provide various degrees of feathering, and for this example the strongest setting was used.

Figure 4.16 shows the result obtained using elliptical cropping with strong feathering. The first point to note is that, as pointed out previously, the image is still rectangular despite the elliptical cropping. The picture has been cropped to a rectangle that is large enough to comfortably hold the ellipse, and the area outside the ellipse has simply been left as white space. The feathering has produced a "soft" edge to the ellipse. Near the edge of the ellipse the image is actually a mixture of the original image and the white background. The image therefore steadily fades out at the edge rather than coming to an abrupt end. While this effect is not well suited to all subject matter, it can produce some professional looking results when used sensibly. For comparison purposes, Figure 4.17 shows the rose picture cropped using a heart shape and no feathering.

Fig.4.17 Here a heart shaped mask has been used without feathering

Fig.4.18 A large amount of feathering used in Photoshop Elements

Photoshop and Photoshop Elements both have the ability to use feathering. First the area to crop is selected using any of the normal selection tools, such as the rectangular or elliptical versions of the Marquee tool. Then Feather is chosen from the Select menu, and a feather value of up to 250 pixels is entered in the small dialogue box that appears. The selection can then be copied and pasted to another image or a blank canvas. In the example of Figure 4.18 a feather value of 75 pixels was used and the cropped image was copied to a blank canvas.

Downsizing

In most cases it will not be sufficient to crop images. A reduction in the resolution will be needed in addition to or instead of cropping. Any photo-editing software should enable images to be resized, but it is

Fig.4.19 The screen after the Resize button is operated

important to realise that a digital image has two sizes. There is the size in terms of the number of pixels in each dimension, and there is the physical size in inches, centimetres, or whatever. You will probably encounter a resolution figure as well, such as 300 pixels per inch. This is derived from the physical size and the number of pixels. For example, an image that has 1200 by 800 pixels and a physical size of 6 inches by 4 inches has a resolution of 200 pixels per inch (1200 divided by 6 = 200).

The physical size of an image is clearly important in desktop publishing or when making prints, but it is usually of no consequence in web applications. A web page creation program might use physical image sizes or have the ability to do so, but in most cases it is only the size in pixels that is of importance. The physical size and resolution settings are usually irrelevant.

Using Photo Express, the size of an image in pixels is altered by first operating the Resize button (Figure 4.19). Next the Pixel option is selected from the Unit menu, and then the new Width and Height values are entered in the appropriate textboxes. If the Keep Aspect Ratio button is active,

Fig.4.20 The screen after the image has been shrunk

only a new Width value has to be entered. The program will then use the height value that keeps the aspect ratio as close as possible to its original ratio. It is advisable to use the constraining facility unless you really do need to alter the aspect ratio. Quite small changes to the aspect ratio of an image can sometimes produce some odd looking results. Operating the Apply button makes the new size take effect (Figure 4.20).

Things are equally straightforward using Photoshop Elements. An image is resized by first selecting Resize from the Image menu, and then Image Size from the submenu that appears. This brings up the Image Size dialogue box (Figure 4.21), and here it is important to have the Resample Image checkbox ticked. The Constrain Proportions checkbox should also be ticked if you wish to leave the aspect ratio of the image unaltered. It is then just a matter of changing the Height and (or) Width value in the upper part of the dialogue box and operating the OK button. The image will then be reduced to the newly specified size. In Figure 4.22 the image has been reduced to a width of 350 pixels and the original aspect ratio has been retained.

*Fig.4.21 In Photoshop and Photoshop Elements the Image Size facility
is used to increase or decrease resolution*

It is only fair to point out that odd things can happen when an image is
scaled up or down. There should be no major problems if the
mathematics are simple, and the image has the number of pixels in each
dimension doubled, trebled, halved, or whatever. In rare cases things
can still go slightly awry though. Suppose there is a vertical line in an
image and that the line is just one pixel wide. With the number of pixels
halved in each dimension, leaving the line in the image effectively doubles
its width. Simply removing it might result in an important element of the
image being omitted. Including some pixels and omitting others would
be unlikely to give convincing results either. Large reductions in the
number of pixels will inevitably require some compromises in the fine
detail.

If the number of pixels is reduced by an odd amount such as 0.57 times
in each dimension, the mathematics are not straightforward and
compromises have to be made. Modern image editing programs are
mostly very good at avoiding obvious problems, and are also good at
retaining detail when the number of pixels is reduced. However, there is
no guarantee that the processed image will be entirely glitch free. Low
resolution images are more prone to scaling problems than the high

Fig.4.22 The image has been duly reduced in size

resolution variety, and the lower the final resolution, the greater the chance of a problem occurring.

Controlling compression

Reducing the number of pixels in an image helps to keep file sizes reasonably small, but compression is also needed if really small file sizes are to be achieved. It is a good idea to retain a full-size version of each image at minimal compression, so that you have a high quality copy available in case you need to use the image for something other than web applications. It is therefore a good idea to save the processed image under a different name using the Save As facility. If the image is not already in Jpeg format, choose Jpeg from the Save as Type menu, or its equivalent in the program you are using.

There will usually be some means of varying the amount of Jpeg compression used, and in the case of Photo Express the Options button is operated in order to produce a window that includes a compression control (Figure 4.23). With the more upmarket programs there will often

Fig.4.23 The amount of compression is governed by the slider control

be a choice of three types of compression, but it is probably best to settle for the default setting. This will usually be for "Standard" or "Baseline" compression, which are different names for the same thing.

In Photoshop Elements the control window of Figure 4.24 appears when an image is saved in Jpeg format. As before, a slider control enables the amount of compression to be altered and there are three different types on offer. It is useful to have the Preview checkbox ticked, because changes in the compression settings will then be applied to the image displayed in the main window. Before saving the image, use the Actual Pixels option in the View menu. The image will then be displayed exactly as it will appear in most browsers, making it easier to accurately judge the effect of various amounts of compression.

The optimum amount of compression is a subjective matter. Some images look much the same whether the maximum or minimum amount of compression is used, while others show adverse effects with even small amounts of compression applied. Simply settling for a standard amount of compression for all web images will not provide optimum results for each image, and a subjective judgement has to be made for

171

Fig.4.24 Photoshop Elements also has a compression control

each one. It is a matter of using as much compression as possible without the image undergoing what you deem to be an unacceptable loss of detail, or it showing any obvious signs of artefacts.

Some image editing programs helpfully show the size of the file that will be produced using the current compression setting. This information is provided in the Size section of the Jpeg Options window of Photoshop Elements, which also shows the typical download time for the image. By default the download time is for a 56k modem, but other options are available from the menu. It is probably best to work on the basis of a 56k modem, since earlier types are now obsolete, and relatively few users have broadband Internet connections. Ideally, web image files should be no more than about 30 kilobytes and only a very few images should be used on each page. Even if an entire page has just 100 kilobytes of data, it would still take 20 seconds or so to download using a real-world 56k Internet connection.

Some image editing programs have a facility specifically for optimising images for web use, although this facility usually just duplicates features that are available elsewhere in the program. However, you may prefer to

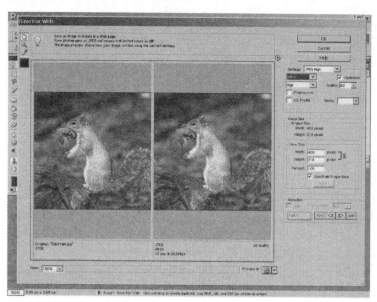

Fig.4.25 The Save For Web facility of Photoshop Elements

have everything conveniently grouped together in a single control panel. Photoshop Elements has the Save For Web option, and this produces the window shown in Figure 4.25. Here the size of the image can be changed, the amount of Jpeg compression can be altered, and so on. Two panels show "before" and "after" versions of the image so that you can see the effects of any changes made. Other file formats can be chosen, but unless there is a good reason to use a different format it is best to save the image as a Jpeg type.

Sharpening

Most image editing software has at least one sharpening filter which is designed to make slightly "soft" images look "crisp" and sharp. This type of filtering is often applied to web images regardless of whether the focus is good or slightly "soft". One reason for using this type of filtering is that an image which looked very sharp and had plenty of detail in its original form is unlikely to look as good in low resolution web form. Detail is lost when the resolution of an image is reduced, and this tends to be perceived as a loss of sharpness. Another reason is simply that

Fig.4.26 The Focus facility of Photo Express 3.0 provides sharpening

emphasising the detail in any image, but particularly a low resolution type, tends to give it a bit more "sparkle". An image that is otherwise a bit dull and "flat" can often be made to look much livelier by adding some sharpening.

The degree of control that can be exercised over the sharpening process varies considerably from one program to another. Many image editing programs only provide preset sharpening where the user has no control over the effect obtained. In Photo Express sharpening can be added by operating the Auto Enhance button and then selecting Focus from the buttons down the right-hand side of the screen (Figure 4.26). This produces a worthwhile increase in sharpness, but something a bit less subtle is often better for web use.

Photoshop Elements has preset and adjustable sharpening filters and it seems to be the equal of the full version of Photoshop in this respect. There are four types of sharpening available from the Sharpen submenu, and the first of these is the straightforward Sharpen option. This operates by looking for variations in colour and tone, and it increases the contrast between adjacent pixels where suitable variations are found. All simple methods of image sharpening use essentially the same method, and are really just providing localised increases in contrast. This can give the illusion of greater sharpness, and I suppose that in a way the image is genuinely sharper, but missing detail can not be put back in by sharpness filtering.

Fig.4.27 The original version of the image

The photograph of the squirrel actually has reasonable sharpness, but for some reason much of the detail in the fur does not stand out as clearly as it might. Also, the reduction in resolution has left the image looking something less than "pin sharp", especially the squirrel's tail which has lost some of its "bite". Figure 4.28 shows the effect of using the Sharpen

Fig.4.28 The image with sharpening applied

filter. For comparison purposes, Figure 4.27 shows the image without any sharpness filtering applied. The change is something less than dramatic, but as viewed on the screen of my monitor anyway, there is a definite improvement in the apparent sharpness of the image, particularly in the fur on the tail. The effect of the Sharpen filter is relatively mild, but and it was probably designed more for printing than for web use. It is useful for web images that are quite sharp but where you feel a little extra "bite" is needed.

Fig.4.29 The image with Sharpen and Sharpen Edges filtering applied

Photoshop Elements can provide stronger or additional filtering. The Sharpen Edges filter, as its name implies, is primarily intended for giving more clearly defined edges, such as the edges of furniture, buildings, and the petals of flowers. This it does very well, but when used in conjunction with the Sharpen filter it will often give a useful improvement in the general sharpness without taking things "over the top". Figure 4.29 shows the squirrel photograph with the Sharpen and Sharpen Edges filtering applied.

There is only a subtle difference between this and the version that only has the Sharpen filtering applied, but the combined effect filtering is quite impressive with the image viewed on a monitor in the Actual Pixels mode. Unlike the original image, it looks acceptably sharp and it still looks quite natural. Large amounts of sharpening can be applied by using the Sharpen filer two or three times, or by using the Sharpen More filter. Figure 4.30 shows the image with the original sharpening removed and the Sharpen More filter applied.

Fig.4.30 The image with the Sharpen More filtering applied

In this case using the Sharpen More filter has produced a quite impressive end result, but with some images its effect is somewhat less impressive. It can add a slightly "brittle" and artificial look with patterns of light pixels appearing in places, and it is often "over the top" when used with high resolution images that will be printed. With low resolution web images it is less likely to take things too far, but it has to be used sensibly. It is advisable to use less extreme filtering when the Sharpen More filter gives an image an unnatural look. Using anything beyond the Sharpen More filter more or less guarantees some rather odd looking results with most images.

Unsharp Mask

The three types of sharpness filtering described so far are handy for those needing a quick and easy solution to a slightly blurred image or wishing to give a sharp image more "bite". However, they provide no real control over the filtering. The same is not true of the Unsharp Mask filter, which has three controls and a preview option (Figure 4.31). The

177

*Fig.4.31 The Unsharp Mask filter gives plenty of control over
          the filtering*

top control is used to set the required amount of filtering, and it covers a range of 1 to 500 percent. A Radius value is set using the middle control, and this controls the number of surrounding pixels that are altered by the sharpening. It is normally necessary to use a low value here in order to obtain an acceptable effect. A low value is particularly important with an image such as the one used here, which has masses of fine detail. A high value tends to give a glowing effect around the edges of objects or where there is a lot of fine detail, and it can also produce oversaturated colours. Set the value too low and no significant sharpening is obtained.

The third slider control sets the Threshold, which is the difference needed between pixels before the sharpening will be applied. High values result in Photoshop finding few areas to sharpen. With a low value the filtering is applied almost everywhere on the image, which usually results in patterns of dots starting to emerge from previously plain areas of the image. It can take a fair amount of juggling with the three controls in order to obtain the best results, but it should be possible to obtain a reasonably sharp looking picture provided the original image contains an adequate amount of detail. Figure 4.32 shows the squirrel photograph

Fig.4.32 The image processed using the Unsharp Mask filter

after processing using the Unsharp Mask filter. This is perhaps a fraction over the top, but it shows the type of improvement that can be achieved.

Many professional users head straight for the Unsharp Mask filter when editing any image. No matter how sharp an image is to start with, it is always possible to make it look "crisper" using this facility, or the similar facilities available in other image editing programs. Whether it is desirable to do so is another matter. For low definition images that will be used on the Internet there is perhaps a good case to be made for emphasising the fine details which might otherwise be lost. The subtle approach often produces rather "flat" results with low definition web images. I habitually use sharpening on web images, but not images that will be printed. There is no harm in trying a sharpening filter on every image, and I would certainly recommend this approach with web images, but there is no point in applying the filtering unless you genuinely like the effect. Try to avoid going through a set routine each time a web image is processed. The best results are produced by tailoring the processing to suit each image.

Background image

Web pages often have a background image instead of a plain background. The image can be large enough to fill the page, or a small image can be "tiled" so that it covers the page. Background images can be very effective when used sensibly, but they normally have to be used in a highly watered down form. Using a normal image tends to give problems with the image dominating the page and distracting the user from the content. Another potential problem is that some of the content tends to blend into the background, making text difficult to read for example.

Fig.4.33 The normal version of the image

Background images generally work best when they are much paler than normal and have low contrast. In other words, they have the opposite requirements of normal images, where strong colours and high contrast are usually of prime importance. A background image that is faded to the point where it is barely recognisable will often work quite well, but one with strong colours and contrast is unlikely to give good results. Also, background images often look stronger once you have added some of the content to the page.

Consequently, it is better to err on the side of caution and make background images quite pale. Although it might look initially as though you have overdone the processing, it will probably look all right once the page has been completed. There is no real problem if the image does not look right once the page is finished. If necessary, a background image that looks too strong or too pale can be erased from the page. The image file can then be processed some more and reapplied to the page.

Ordinary brightness and contrast controls are all that are needed in order to produce a pale image for use as a background. Figure 4.33 shows a

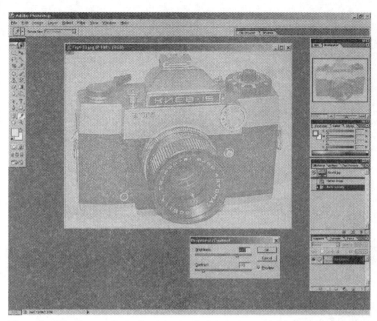

Fig.4.34 The image faded using the Brightness and Contrast controls

picture of a camera that will be processed for use as a background image, and Figure 4.34 shows the image being processed in Photoshop 7. The same controls are present in Photoshop Elements and just about every other image editing program. Start by reducing the contrast to produce a suitably subdued image. This might be sufficient to produce the desired effect, but in general the image looks too dark unless the brightness is boosted as well. A little juggling with the two controls should soon produce an image having the required characteristics.

Most if not all images will be too large to be used as a tiled background, and they will therefore have to be reduced in size using the normal method. In order to work well it is usually necessary to reduce the image to a very small size so that there are a large number of tiles on the page. In terms of pixels it is best to aim for no more than about 100 on the largest dimension. Best results are obtained with a tightly cropped image of a single object, like the camera image of Figure 4.33. It is then easy to see what the image is depicting even when the resolution is very low. When an image is used in tiled form it is still important to use a faded version that will add atmosphere without dominating the page.

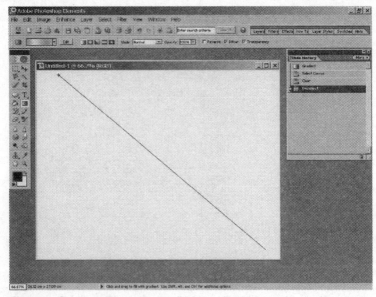

Fig.4.35 Gradient fills are controlled by a line dragged onto the screen

*Fig.4.36 The fill produced by the control
line above*

Generating backgrounds

The more sophisticated image editing programs have the ability to produce images from scratch, with the user "painting" the image onto the screen. In the hands of a skilled artist this can be a very effective method of producing backgrounds, but the results produced by dabblers are often less impressive. It is still possible to produce some good backgrounds without an abundance of artistic talent, and the gradient fill capability of some image editing programs provide a simple means of producing good backgrounds. Some web page creation programs have a similar facility.

The Gradient tool of Photoshop Elements is used to produce gradient fills. Of course, you must first produce a blank image to fill, and the first step is to select New from the File menu. Then add the

Fig.4.37 A gradient fill produced using the Angle mode

appropriate dimensions into the Width and Height textboxes and operate the OK button. A gradient is placed on the blank image by dragging a line onto the screen, as in Figure 4.35. The angle of the gradient is governed by the angle of the line, and the gradient is spread out over the

length of the line. The areas beyond each end of the line are set at the start and finish colours of the gradient.

Figure 4.36 shows the gradient fill that was generated using the control line and settings of Figure 4.35. This was produced using the Linear Gradient, but four other types of gradient are available via the buttons on the

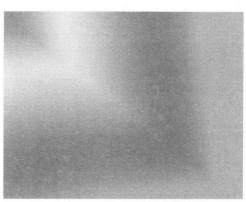

Fig.4.38 A Diamond mode gradient fill

Options bar. Figures 4.37 and 4.38 respectively show fills produced using the Angle and Diamond gradient options. The pattern of the default gradient is shown in the pattern button near the left end of the Options bar, but there is a drop-down menu here that offers further patterns. Several variations are available from each type of gradient by altering

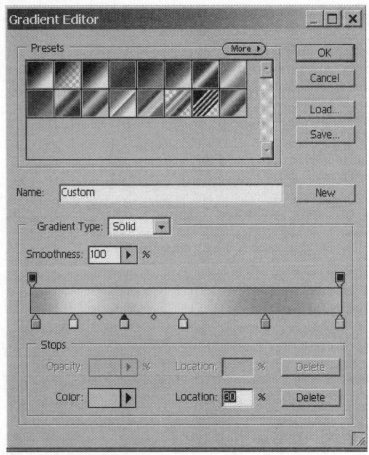

Fig.4.39 The Gradient Editor enables practically any gradient to be produced

the position, length, and angle of the control line, so it is worthwhile experimenting a little.

A pattern can be customised by selecting it and then left-clicking on the pattern button. This brings up the Gradient Editor (Figure 4.39), which shows the current pattern using what is effectively a larger version of the pattern button. Left-click below the gradient bar in order to add a new colour at that point on the bar. The markers beneath the bar can be slid into new positions so it is easy to make fine adjustments to the

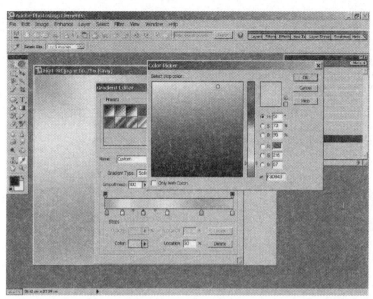

Fig.4.40 The colours at the control points can be changed using the Color Picker

graduations. A marker can be removed by left-clicking on it to select it and then operating the Delete button. Alternatively, just drag it away from the gradient bar. The colour provided by a marker can be altered using the Eyedropper tool to select a colour from an image.

To mix a colour, select the appropriate marker and then left-click the colour button near the bottom left-hand corner of the window. Alternatively, double-click the appropriate marker. Either way, the standard Color Picker will be launched (Figure 4.40) and the

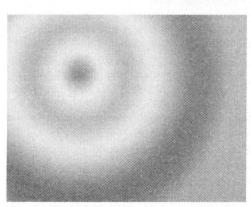

Fig.4.41 The fill produced by the settings of Fig.4.39

Fig.4.42 The "straight" version of the photograph

required colour can then be selected in the usual way. When a marker is selected, a smaller marker appears on each side it. These minor markers control the point at which the middle colours occur, and they can be dragged to new positions to distort the graduations. With the Smoothness setting at 100 percent there is the usual gradual and smooth change from one colour to the next. With lower settings there is a faster rate of change close to each of the main markers. Figure 4.41 shows a radial gradient produced using the Gradient Editor settings shown in Figure 4.39.

If you would like backgrounds that have the painted or sketched look but lack the ability to draw or paint them, there is an easy way of producing suitable artwork. The more capable image editing programs have various types of filtering available, including so-called artistic filters. The idea of these filters is to process a photograph to make it look like a sketch, engraving, watercolour, or whatever. Photoshop Elements has a wide

Fig.4.43 The simplified image produce by the filtering

range of artistic and sketching filters. The difference between the two is that the sketch filters produce monochrome results whether the source images are colour or monochrome types. Artistic filters produced images that retain the source mode, and will therefore produce colour images from suitable source material.

The sketch filters actually produce some of the best results for use as backgrounds. The image of Figure 4.42 was processed using the Note-Paper filter to produce the image of Figure 4.43. Although the result is a greyscale image, provided it was originally a colour image it will still be in the original colour mode. It can therefore be tinted any desired colour using the colour balance controls. If necessary, the brightness and contrast controls can then be used to make the image suitably pale. It is certainly worthwhile experimenting with any artistic or sketching facilities if your image editing software has them. Some top-notch backgrounds can be produced in this way.

Indexed Color

Photoshop Elements, like many image editing programs, has more than one colour mode. One of these modes is called Indexed Color. This mode is used when the final output will be to a device that supports a relatively limited range of colours. These days most monitors and printers support a huge colour range, making the Indexed Color mode of relatively little practical use. In modern computing its main application is in the production of web images. There is a potential problem when mixing web colours, which is simply that colours produced on one computer, could be somewhat different when displayed on another computer. One reason for this is that different monitors produce different colours from the same colour values. In actual fact, the same monitor will produce different colours depending on how it is set up.

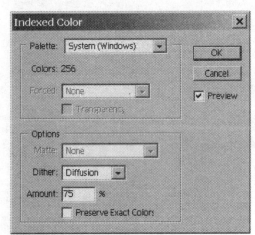

Fig.4.44 The Indexed Color window

A second problem is that not all computers have the same colour capabilities. The main problem here is differences between Macintosh computers and PCs. There can be differences between computers of the same general type, and some PCs have simple graphics cards offering relatively few colours, while others have graphics systems that can handle millions of different colours. However, this is not a major problem these days as even budget PCs and most laptops tend to have good graphics capabilities.

It is the Macintosh and PC differences that are of prime concern to most web page designers. There is no point in them worrying about poorly adjusted monitors, since there is nothing web designers can do about it. The Macintosh/PC problem is different. There is a set of so-called "browser safe" or "web safe" colours that can be reproduced by the popular Microsoft and Netscape browsers in both their Windows and Macintosh versions. Using these 200 or so colours does not guarantee that precisely the specified colour will be produced on every computer, but it does at least keep the inevitable divergences to a minimum.

A small dialogue box like the one in Figure 4.44 appears when the Indexed Color mode is selected. In this example Photoshop Elements is running on a PC, so it is the Windows system colours that are offered by default. Various options are available from the Palette menu though (Figure 4.45), and it is the Web option that provides the web safe colours. If you try converting a colour photograph to this mode it will probably not look much different after the conversion. This is perhaps a little surprising when one considers that the maximum number of colours on the screen has probably been reduced from millions to just 216.

The reason for the lack of change is that Photoshop Elements uses dithering in an attempt minimise any change in appearance. In other words, it is relying on optical mixing in the viewer's eye to effectively merge adjacent pixels

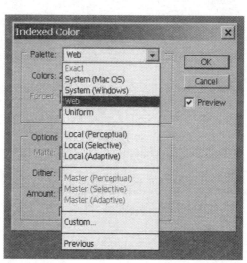

Fig.4.45 The Web mode is selected

to produce additional colours. Zooming in will often reveal the dithering, with the smooth changes in colour being replaced by a noticeable pattern. Figures 4.46 and 4.47 respectively show close-up "before" and "after" views of a photograph. Although the dithering is obvious on close inspection, it is usually something less than obvious with the image viewed at normal size, which is really all you need to be concerned about with web images.

When using the Indexed Color mode with web safe colours, the Color Picker will not automatically limit the selection to web safe colours (Figure

Fig.4.46 The normal version of the photograph, which uses a full range of colours and no dithering

4.48). However, it will do so if the Only Web Colors checkbox near the bottom left-hand corner of the window is ticked. Whether it is worth bothering with web safe colours when producing photographic images is debatable. Slightly improved colour accuracy may well be obtained, but only at the expense of somewhat grainier images. This is a subjective matter that you have to judge for yourself. I prefer not to bother with web safe colours for images that will be used on the Internet. The web safe colours are probably a better bet when selecting text and background colours. The range of 216 colours should be sufficient to obtain any desired look, and you can be reasonably sure that the colours will be displayed as expected on the vast majority of computers.

Fig.4.47 This version uses web safe colours with dithering

File conversion

Most web images are in Jpeg format, but there are two other standard web formats. These are the GIF and Png file formats.

GIF

The full name for this format is CompuServe Graphics Interchange Format, and programs that use it have to be licensed by CompuServe. It is in widespread use on the Internet. However, this format is generally preferred for line art such as graphs and most diagrams, cartoons, or practically any non-photographic images. In fact the GIF image format is sometimes used for monochrome photographs, and it can handle colour photographs. The limited colour range makes it a dubious choice for colour photographs though. These days Jpeg is the more popular

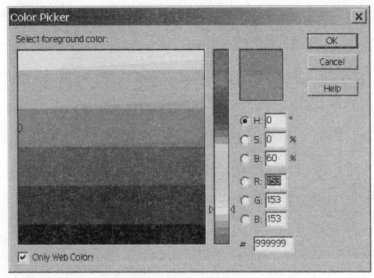

Fig.4.48 The Photoshop Color Picker in the web safe mode

choice for images of this type. Consequently, and despite its web compatibility, you are unlikely to have any need for the GIF format unless you use non-photographic images on your site. GIF files can handle simple animations, but for anything more than simple animations a different format such Flash is required, together with a suitable media player.

Png

This is a relatively new file format for images, and it is apparently pronounced pong, as in nasty smell or Ping-Pong. Png stands for Portable Network Graphic. It is designed to be a sort of universal licence-free image format that will eventually replace the GIF format. It combines small file sizes with the ability to use an unlimited colour range. Although relatively new, any reasonably modern browser should be able to handle Png images (Internet Explorer 4 or later for example). However, it is less universal than either the Jpg or GIF formats. Png is a technically competent format that can handle colour photographs well, but it seems unlikely that it will topple the well established Jpeg format as the standard for colour photographs on the Internet.

There is usually no great problem if you have an image in a non-web compatible format that you wish to use in a web page. You can actually buy image file conversion programs, but this will not usually be necessary. Provided an image will load into your image editing program it should be possible to save the image in a web compatible format.

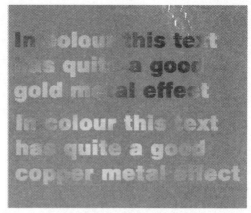

Fig.4.49 Gradient fills can give metallic effects

All but the most basic of image editing programs can load images in a useful range of file formats, and save them in Jpeg, GIF, or Png format. This enables them to operate as image file conversion programs. At one time using any form of file conversion process more or less guaranteed that errors would occur, and converting image files was probably the most problematic form of conversion. Fortunately, things are much better these days. Vector graphics (most charts, diagrams, etc.) can still be troublesome, but conversions involving digital photographs are usually very straightforward and trouble free.

Large text

As explained previously, headlines in fancy fonts and (or) with clever effects are often created using a graphics program. A finished headline is saved as an ordinary Jpeg file and placed on the web page just like any other image. The advantage of this system is that the text will be displayed correctly even if the correct font is not installed on visitors' computers. By no means all image editing programs are blessed with good text facilities, and one of the more sophisticated programs is required for this type of thing. A paint program should also be able to produce fancy text, as should any illustration program.

Producing fancy text with a graphics program is not just a matter of using the exotic fonts installed on your PC. With a good graphics program it is possible to add various special effects to text. With Photoshop and Photoshop Elements for example, it is possible to have text in the form

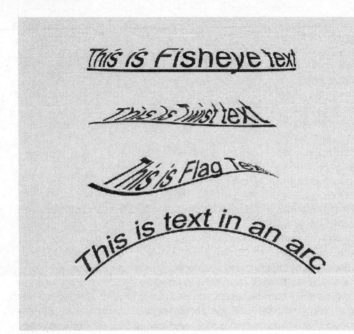

Fig.4.50 Four examples of warped text

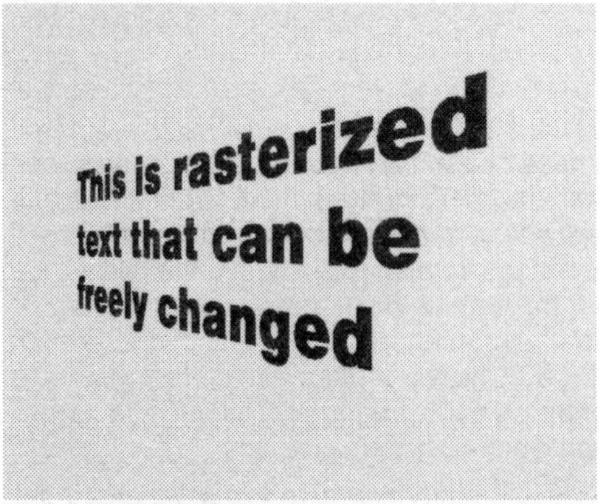

Fig.4.51 Rasterized text can be freely distorted
and filtered

of a selection that can be given gradient fills. This method has been used in Figure 4.49, which gives quite a good shiny metal effect in its original colour form. Photographs can also be used to provide the fill for this type of text.

There are often facilities to distort text in various ways. Photoshop and Photoshop Elements

Fig.4.52 Drop shadow text is popular for use on web sites

have a Warp Text facility that can provide a wide range of distortions, a few of which are shown in Figure 4.50. There are controls that enable the distortions to be tailored to suit your requirements. It is often possible to skew text in much the same way as images can be skewed to correct or add perspective effects. With text the idea is usually to add a sort of 3D effect, as in Figure 4.51. Note that the text usually has to be converted to a bitmap before it can be distorted. This process is sometimes termed rasterizing, and once text has been converted to a bitmap it is no longer possible to edit it using the text editing facilities. However, the full range of image editing facilities becomes available. Make sure there are no errors before the text is converted.

Some programs have a facility for producing special effects such as drop shadows and glowing effects. Even where they are not available it is not too difficult to produce your own effects. The drop shadow effect of Figure 4.52 was produced by copying the original text, offsetting the copy slightly from the original, lightening it, and then adding some blur filtering. Using copying and filtering techniques it is possible to produce numerous interesting effects. It is well worth experimenting with a good graphics program to see what text effects you can come up with.

Finally

Producing web images is a complete subject in its own right, but the basic techniques described in this chapter are all that is needed in order to produce effective web images. Probably the most important point is to make sure that files sizes of web images are kept as small as possible. Make the size (in pixels) no larger than is really necessary, and apply as much compression as you dare.

Points to remember

Digital images are comprised of thousands or even millions of tiny dots, or pixels as they are termed. High resolution is normally regarded as an advantage, but the large file sizes associated with high resolution images makes them undesirable for most web applications. Images of around 400 by 300 pixels are more than adequate for normal web use. Many web images are significantly smaller than this.

Using low resolution images means that the amount of detail in each image will be strictly limited. Avoid the temptation to use complex images that in low resolution form look like nothing much at all. Tightly cropping the subject helps to optimise use of the available resolution.

While using compression is definitely not going to improve the image quality, it does not necessarily produce a significant degradation either. Reducing the amount of data by a factor of around three or four is unlikely to produce any significant reduction in quality. In fact the quality is generally very good with compression ratios of up to about eight to one. Going beyond this is almost certain to produce an obvious reduction in image quality. The dividing line between acceptable compression and too much is a subjective matter.

The purpose of a background image is to provide atmosphere without detracting from the subject matter. An image will normally have to be made much paler if it is to be used effectively as a background. This is just a matter of using the ordinary brightness and contrast controls to greatly reduce the contrast and then set the required brightness.

Small images used to provide tiled backgrounds are often very effective. This type of thing works best with a small image and lots of "tiles". This generally means using an image that is no more than about 100 pixels on its longest dimension. The contrast still has to be greatly reduced in order to prevent the background from distracting viewers from the main subject matter.

You do not have to be an artistic genius in order to produce effective backgrounds having the painted look. Gradient fills can be used to almost instantly produce attractive backgrounds. Many image editing programs have filters that will effectively convert a photograph into a sketch or painting. Filtered images can produce some extremely effective background designs.

There are 216 so-called "web safe" colours that should be produced accurately on properly adjusted Macintosh and Windows computers. Whether it is worth limiting photographic images to this limited colour set is debatable. The advantages could be outweighed by the drawbacks. There is perhaps a better argument for using these colours for text and backgrounds.

File conversion programs can be used to convert practically any image file into a web compatible format (Jpeg, Png, and GIF). However, most image editing software can import images in a wide range of formats and save them in a web compatible format. Consequently, a separate file conversion program is usually unnecessary.

Many graphics programs are capable of producing fancy text that can be as large as you like. The text can be saved in Jpeg format and then loaded into a web page like any other image. The text will be displayed correctly even if users' computers are not equipped with the correct font.

4   Web graphics

Web creation software

Word processor

If you prefer to use the conventional approach to web site production rather than the web publishing route there are plenty of ways in which web pages can be produced. Such is the importance of the Internet these days that practically every program seems to be able to export documents in HTML format. However, the fact that a program can export files in this format does not necessarily mean it is well suited to the production of web sites.

Most programs that can produce HTML pages should be suitable for producing single page sites, but they are less than ideal for anything more complex. A program designed for site building provides some help with linking the pages on your local site, and keeping then linked when they are uploaded. With most other programs it is entirely up to you to make sure that the uploaded site links together correctly. This is by no means impossible, but it can be a bit tricky. If you need to produce a multi-page site it is advisable to obtain suitable software, which will not necessarily cost a great deal.

Practically any word processor is sufficient to produce a single page site that does include any graphics. Because it is the most widely used word processor, Microsoft Word 2002 will be used as the basis for this example. Any reasonably modern word processor should be able to produce similar results. The first step is to select New from the File menu, which will produce a set of options down the right-hand side of the screen (Figure 5.1). Left-click the General Templates link near the bottom of the list, and the Templates window will be launched (Figure 5.2). Double-click the Web Page icon, and a blank page will appear in the main section of the window.

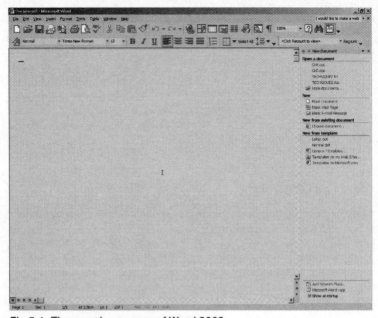

Fig.5.1 The opening screen of Word 2002

It is then just a matter of adding the content in the normal way. The usual text formatting facilities are available, as are horizontal lines, etc. Figure 5.3 shows a dummy page that has some simple text formatting and a couple of horizontal lines added to the heading. A hyperlink can be added by first selecting the text for the link and then choosing Hyperlink from the Insert menu. This produces a window (Figure 5.4) where the usual file browser can be used to select a file on your PC or the URL can be typed into the textbox at the bottom of the window. If required, Alt text can be added into the Text to display textbox. Press the OK button when all the information has been added. The link text will be automatically underlined and changed to the default link colour, which is the usual blue (Figure 5.5).

As with many programs, if you use a web address in the text it will automatically be turned into a hyperlink to that address. There is normally no point in doing so, but a hyperlink can be removed from the text by right-clicking it and then selecting Remove Hyperlink from the pop-up menu. Like any hyperlink in Word, the link can be edited by right-clicking it and selecting Edit Hyperlink from the popup menu.

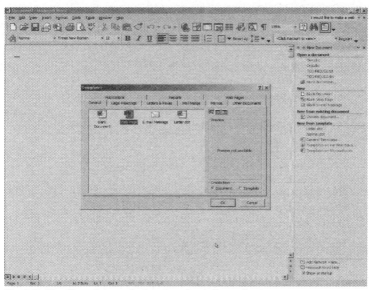

Fig.5.2 The Templates window has been launched

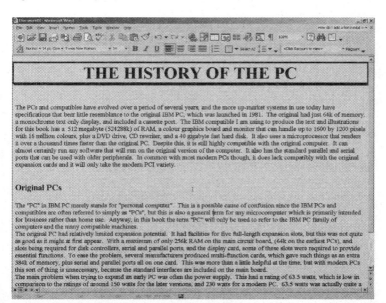

Fig.5.3 A simple text-only page in Word 2002

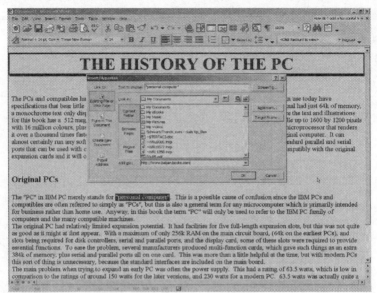

Fig.5.4 A form of file browser is used to add a link

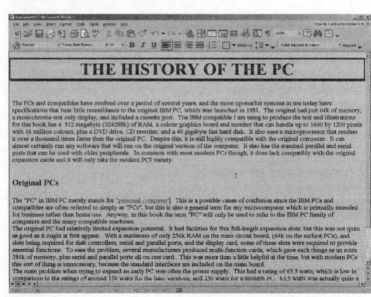

Fig.5.5 The link text has been underlined and changed to blue

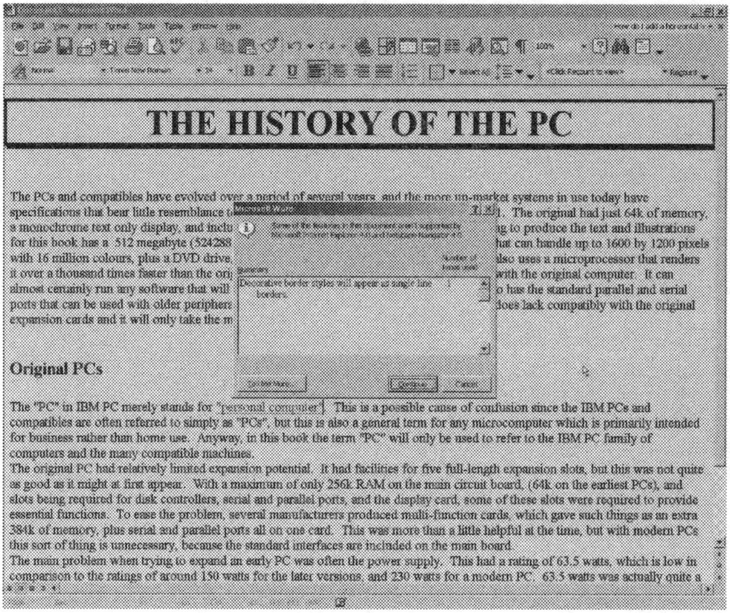

Fig.5.6 A warning message might appear when the page is saved

When the page is saved to disc there might be a warning message (Figure 5.6) explaining that certain features of the page will not be displayed properly on older browsers. Any problems of this type are unlikely to be of any real significance, so go ahead and save the page. When the dummy page was tried in Internet Explorer it followed the original layout quite accurately (Figure 5.7). The drop shadow has disappeared from the heading, but there are no other differences of note. Operating the link to the Babani Books site worked correctly (Figure 5.8).

Pictures

Of course, with Word and many other modern word processors it is possible to add pictures to pages. Most word processors, including Word, also have word wrapping facilities. This makes it possible to go beyond simple text-only web pages. Figure 5.9 shows the dummy web page with a photograph added. Note that Word will automatically produce a subfolder having the same name as the HTML page but with "_files" added at the end. This will be used to store copies of any support files

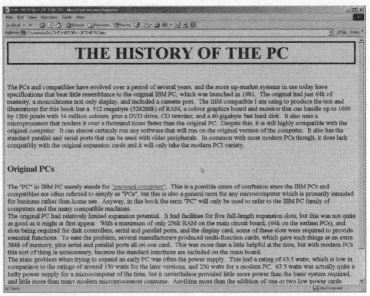

Fig.5.7 The page layout is produced quite accurately in Internet Explorer

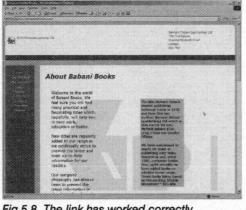

Fig.5.8 The link has worked correctly

needed by the page, including any image types. Figure 5.10 shows the revised dummy page displayed in Internet Explorer, and things have not gone quite right. This can happen with any HTML page, but things are more likely to slip out of place when images are used. A little editing of the page will usually sort things out, and in this case a couple of extra carriage returns produced much better results (Figure 5.11).

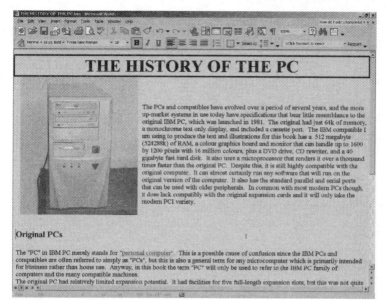

Fig.5.9 The dummy page with a picture added

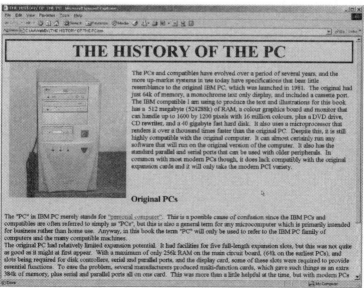

Fig.5.10 The page has not worked properly in a browser

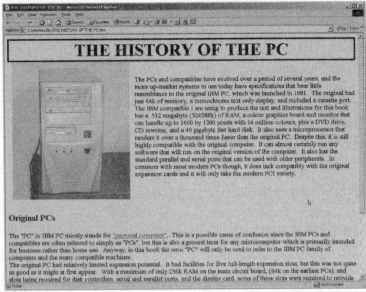

Fig.5.11 After a few minor adjustments the page displays correctly in Internet Explorer

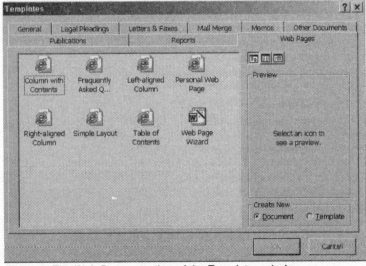

Fig.5.12 The Web Pages section of the Templates window

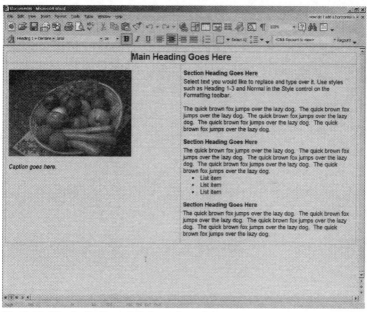

Fig.5.13 The Left-aligned Column template

The template used to produce the dummy page was really little more than a blank page, but there are a few more helpful templates available. These are accessed by going through the same initial steps but the Web Pages tab is operated when the Templates window is reached. This produces several templates to choose from (Figure 5.12), and the one shown in Figure 5.13 is the Left-aligned Column template. In standard web template fashion, the existing content indicates the type of real content that it should be replaced with. Of course, the photograph on the left should also be deleted and replaced with your selected image. Figure 5.14 shows the page with some content added and Figure 5.15 shows the page displayed in Internet Explorer. This time the page layout has been reproduced quite accurately in Internet Explorer and no editing was required.

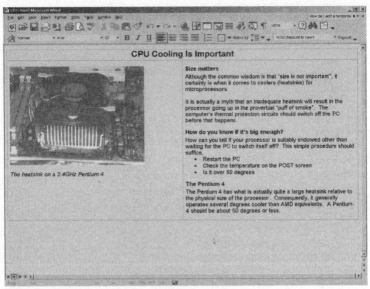

Fig.5.14 The template with some real content added

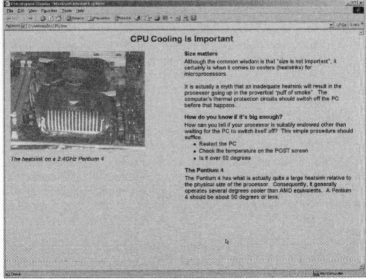

Fig.5.15 The page has been displayed correctly by Internet Explorer

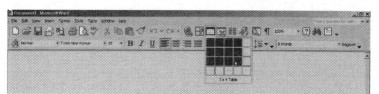

Fig.5.16 Adding a table using the Table button

Tables

Word has a table facility that can be accessed via the appropriate button on the toolbar (Figure 5.16). For more complex tables and a range of options select Insert from the Table menu, followed by Table from the submenu. The Insert Table dialogue box (Figure 5.17) can then be used to set the required parameters for the table. In Figure 5.18 a four column by three row table has been added. As usual, the cells will expand to fit the content you add to them. In Figure 5.19 some photographs and captions have been added to the table, and a heading has been placed above it.

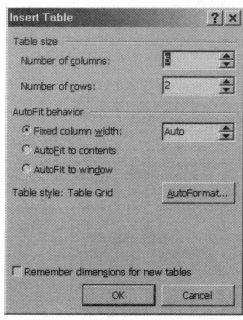

Fig.5.17 The Insert Table window

A photograph can be selected by left-clicking on it, and it is then possible to resize it by dragging the handles that appear.

A floating toolbar offering some basic editing facilities appears when an image is selected, but where possible it is best to do all the image editing in a separate program prior to loading the images. Figure 5.20 shows

Fig.5.18 A four column by three row table added to the page

Fig.5.19 Some content added to the cells

Fig.5.20 The page has displayed correctly in Internet Explorer

the finished page displayed in Internet Explorer, and the layout of the Word version has been accurately retained.

Word is not limited to straightforward tables, and there is an option to draw tables onto the screen. This facility is accessed by selecting Draw Table from the Table menu, and this produces a floating toolbar (Figure 5.21). Using the tools this provides it is possible to drag cells onto screen, change the fill colour, and so on. There are some restrictions on the size and placement of cells, but you are not limited to a regular table. Where necessary the cells will expand to fit the content, and then resized by dragging the cell walls. Figure 5.22 shows a deliberately haphazard layout in Word, and Figure 5.23 shows how this has been correctly carried through when the page is viewed using a browser.

In order to add an image to a cell it is just a matter of placing the text cursor in the appropriate cell, selecting Picture from the Insert menu, followed by From File from the submenu that appears. The standard file browser is then used to select the correct image file. The same method is used to add an image direct onto a page, but the text cursor is placed at the appropriate point on the page prior to inserting the image. In

Fig.5.21　Table cells can be drawn onto the screen

Fig.5.22　A deliberately haphazard layout using table cells

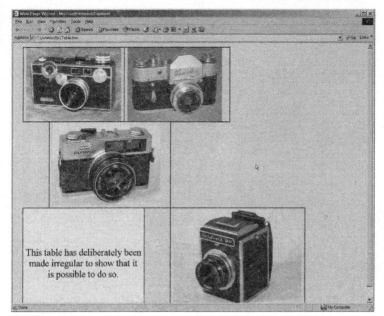

This table has deliberately been
made irregular to show that it
is possible to do so.

*Fig.5.23 The layout has been reproduced quite accurately in a
browser*

general, the table method provides a more controllable and accurate
means of placing images.

Web wizard

Word is rather more capable than most programs that are not specifically
designed for creating web sites. It is not the ideal tool for the job, but it
can be used to produce complex web pages or even complete web
sites. If you intend to go beyond a single web page it is worth considering
the Web Page Wizard. This is included as an option in the web page
templates, and the window of Figure 5.24 appears when this option is
selected. This is just a welcome message and construction of the web
site begins at the next window (Figure 5.25). Here you name the site
and specify the folder where the new site should be saved, or simply
accept the defaults.

Operating the Next button moves things on to the next window (Figure
5.26), and here the required type of navigation is selected. The site will
use a navigation frame, and the first option gives a navigation frame

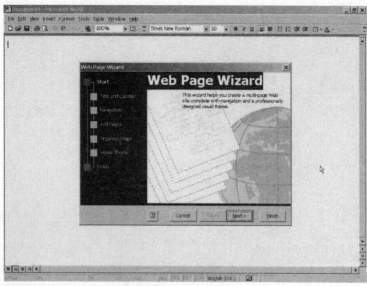

Fig.5.24 The initial window of the Web Page Wizard

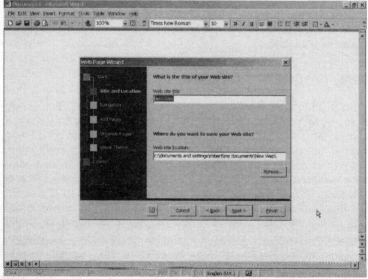

Fig.5.25 The site is named and stored in the specified folder

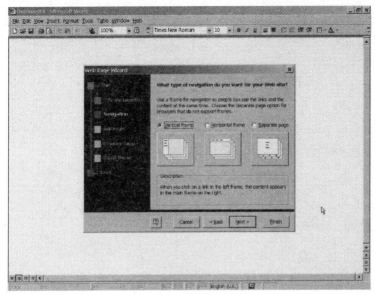

Fig.5.26 Here the navigation layout is chosen

down the left-hand side of the screen. The middle option produces a navigation bar at the top of the screen, and the final option uses a separate page for navigation. Choose the required number of pages at the next window (Figure 5.27), which will produce a homepage and two blank pages by default. Operate the Add New Blank Page button to add each additional page you require. It is also possible to add a page based on one of the installed templates. Operate the Add Template Page and then select the required template from the list that appears. A page can be deleted by selecting it and operating the Remove Page button.

At the next page (Figure 5.28) it is possible to change the order of the pages. To move a page, first left-click its entry in the list and then operate the Move Up and Move Down buttons. Next a theme is chosen, which actually means choosing a background design (Figure 5.29). A theme will be used by default, but a radio button gives the option of not bothering with one. The default theme can be replaced with a different one by operating the Browse Themes button and then choosing a theme from the list that appears (Figure 5.30). Note that some of them are not installed on the computer by default and the installation CD-ROM is needed in order to use any of these themes.

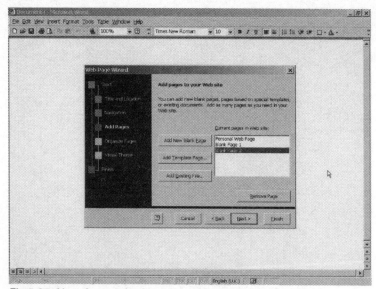

Fig.5.27 Next the required number of pages is selected

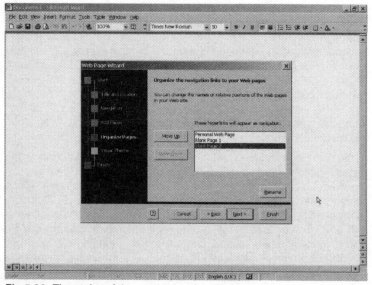

Fig.5.28 The order of the pages can be changed

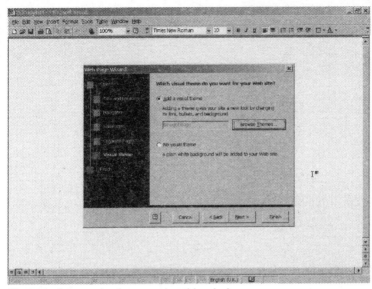

Fig.5.29 A theme is chosen using this window

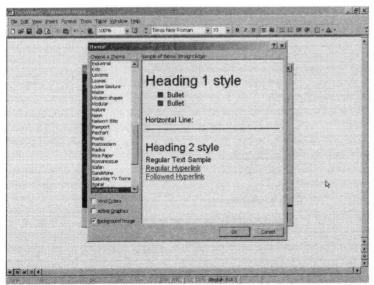

Fig.5.30 The required theme is selected from the large list on the left

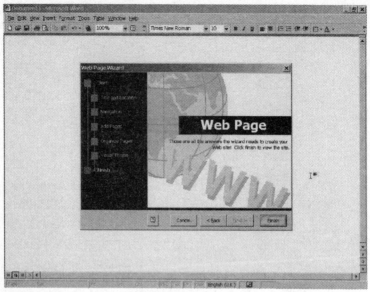

Fig.5.31 This window simply confirms that the site is finished

The real thing

This completes the process, and the next window (Figure 5.31) simply confirms that the site has been generated. The homepage of the site then appears in the main Word window (Figure 5.32). The dummy content is then replaced with your own material. There is no need to get involved with the formatting, since this is already done for you. If you accidentally delete some text, and the formatting that goes with it, just use the Undo facility to reinstate the text and formatting. Of course, it is possible to change any of the existing formatting if you prefer to customise the layout. To edit one of the other pages in the site it is just a matter of operating its link in the navigation frame, and the appropriate page will then appear in the content frame (Figure 5.33).

Word clearly has the ability to go beyond the production of simple web pages, and it is possible to use this program to produce quite sophisticated web sites. It is primarily a word processor though, and the web capability is something of an afterthought. The same basic criticism applies to all programs that are primarily intended for some other application but have the ability to produce web pages or sites. They can

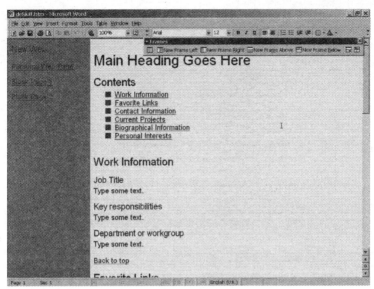

Fig.5.32 The homepage, complete with dummy content

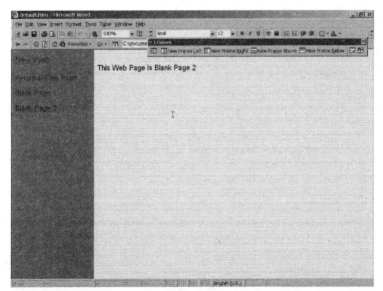

Fig.5.33 Operating the appropriate link brings up page two

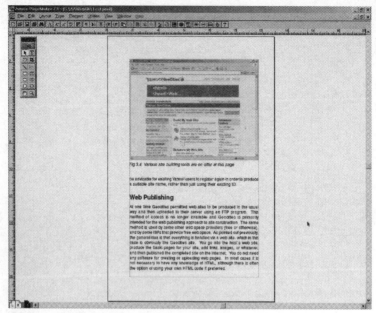

Fig.5.34 The example page in PageMaker 7

not produce web pages with the same ease as a web page creation program, and there is often little or no assistance in combining pages to form a cohesive web site.

Word is rather more capable than most programs that are not specifically designed for producing web sites, and many millions of PCs are already equipped with the program. It is certainly worth considering, if you already have Word on your PC as it is effectively a free web page creation program. However, it is rather less straightforward to use than many out-and-out web creation programs, and you have to bear in mind that some features of Word do not translate well into HTML code. There can always be differences between the original design and the way that a page actually looks when it is displayed via a browser, but there is a greater chance of these divergences occurring when using Word.

Another common criticism of Word is that it does not produce particularly efficient code, although there are programs that can "clean" Word's HTML output. In truth, there are probably relatively few web creation programs that produce really efficient code. Anyway, many consider a good low-

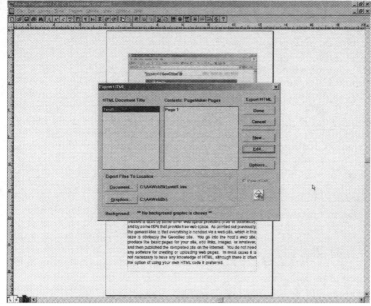

Fig.5.35 The Export HTML window of PageMaker 7

cost web page creation program to be a better option, but if Word is installed on your PC there is nothing to lose by trying it out. You can always move on to another program if Word fails to meet your requirements.

HTML export

If your PC has a desktop publishing program installed then it is virtually certain that it will have a facility to export pages in HTML. It should also have the ability to handle hyperlinks. On the face of it, a program of this type is ideal for producing web pages. In practice the exported pages might lose something in the translation to HTML code. It is the same problem that can occur with Word. Things in the repertoire of the desktop publishing program will not necessarily translate properly into HTML.

Figure 5.34 shows a page in PageMaker 7, and it is the main content from a page of this book. It is easily exported as an HTML page, and it is just a matter of selecting Export from the File menu and HTML from the

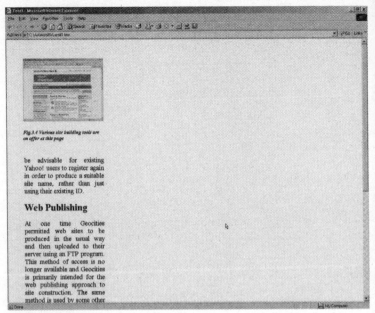

Fig.5.36 The exported page is rather narrow when displayed using
a browser

resultant submenu. This produces the dialogue box of Figure 5.35 where
the folders for the files are chosen and similar parameters are set.
Operating the Export HTML button results in the page being generated,
and Figure 5.36 shows the test page displayed in Internet Explorer. The
graphic has shrunk relative to the text, but the basic layout has been
retained. This has resulted in a narrower but longer version of the page.
This sort of problem can usually be sorted out with a little trial and error,
but most desktop publishing programs are less than ideal for web page
creation. Again, there is no harm in trying out a desktop publishing
program or any other program installed on your PC that has a facility for
producing HTML output. If it fails to live up to expectations you can
always try something else.

Netscape Composer

There are plenty of free web page creation programs available if you do
not already have something suitable installed on your PC. The Netscape
Navigator browser can be obtained for nothing on the Internet

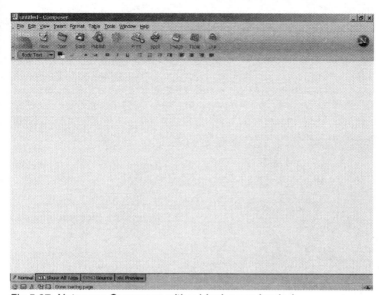

Fig.5.37 Netscape Composer with a blank page loaded

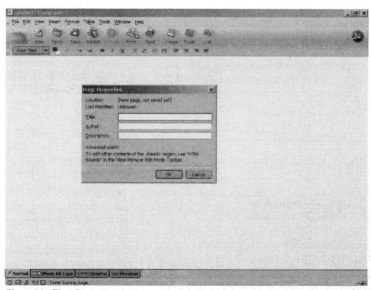

Fig.5.38 The first step is to name the new document

(www.netscape.com), and it is often included on the cover discs of computing magazines. Netscape is actually more than just a browser, and other programs are included with the browser. One of these is Netscape Composer, which is a simple but effective WYSIWYG web creation program. Note that you do not have to use Netscape Navigator as your default browser if you install this package. Your existing browser will work as before provided you make sure that Navigator is not set as the default browser during the installation procedure. With Netscape installed and Composer launched, the opening screen of Figure 5.37 appears.

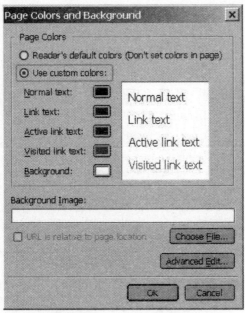

The first step is to give the new document a name, and this is achieved by selecting Page Title and Properties from the Format menu. This produces the window shown in Figure 5.38, where the relevant details are entered. By default the colours for the page will be the defaults of the browser used to display the page, but you can use your own

Fig.5.39 The colours are controlled via this window

colours by selecting Page Colors and Background from the Format menu. This produces the control window of Figure 5.39. Operate the Use Custom Colors radio button and then select the required colours for the background, link text, etc. Operating one of the colour buttons produces a colour swatch so that a new colour can be selected. Alternatively, any colour can be obtained by typing the corresponding HTML colour value into the textbox. A background image can be added by typing the full path and filename into the text box or by selecting the file using the browser.

Fig.5.40 A simple headline added to the page

One way to add a heading for the page is to simply type the text at the top of the page and then format it using the text formatting facilities in the toolbar. The usual alignment options are available including a fully justified option. The full range of heading text sizes is available from the drop-down menu at the left end of the toolbar. The text colour can be changed by selecting the text and operating the upper colour button just to the right of the text size menu. This produces the colour swatch window so that a new colour can be selected. Figure 5.40 shows the page with a headline added using this method.

Basic tables

Netscape Composer supports tables, which gives two options for the headline if the table method is to be used. Either the headline can be placed in a table having just one cell, or tables can be used for the whole page with a wide one at the top being used to accommodate the headline. The headline could still be fitted in its own table if the second method is used, or it could be part of a more complex table.

Adding a table is straightforward, and the easiest way is to operate the Table button. Alternatively, select Insert from the Table menu and then Table from the submenu. Either way the Insert Table window will be launched (Figure 5.41). The number of columns and rows are set via the appropriate text boxes. By default the table's width is set as a percentage of the page width, but the drop-down menu offers the alternative of using a fixed number of pixels. The thickness of the cell walls is set in pixels. Figure 5.42 shows a three by three table produced using the default settings.

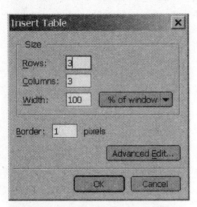

Fig.5.41 The Insert Table window

In Figure 5.43 a headline has been placed in a one by one table. The text cursor was placed at the top of the screen and centre

Fig.5.42 A three column by three row table added to the page

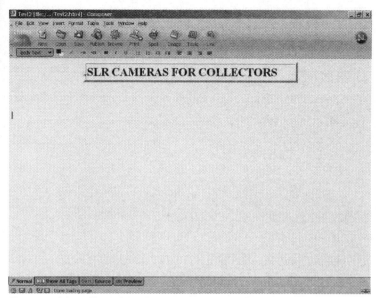

Fig.5.43 A headline placed in a single-cell table

alignment was selected before inserting the table. Accordingly, the table has been horizontally centred rather than being aligned with the left side of the screen. The width of the table was set at 60 percent but in normal table fashion it will, if necessary, expand horizontally and vertically to accommodate the content.

One slight problem is that the text in the cell is aligned with the left wall and not centrally, which mars the overall appearance. The text can be centred by first selecting Table Properties from the Table menu. This launches the Table Properties window (Figure 5.44) where various parameters for the table as a whole can be set. In this case it is the cell properties that must be altered, so the Cell tab is activated. The vertical and horizontal Content Alignment settings should be set at Centre and Middle respectively. Operating the Apply button will then give the heading the correct alignment within the cell (Figure 5.45).

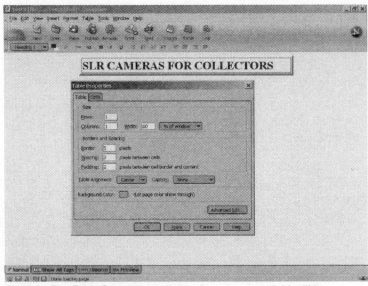

Fig.5.44 The Table Properties window has some useful facilities

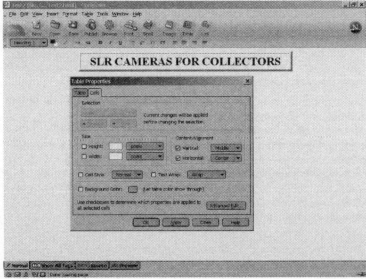

Fig.5.45 Here the text has been properly centred

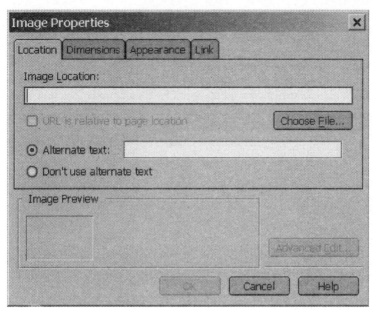

Fig.5.46 An image is selected using the Image Properties window

Adding an image

Next an image will be added to the page on the right-hand side and the accompanying text will be made to wrap around the image to the left and underneath it. A blank line is added below the heading in order to move the image down slightly and away from the heading. The image is then added on the next line using right alignment so that it is aligned with the right side of the page. Next, Image is selected from the Insert menu, and this produces an image browser that enables the required file to be selected, and the Alt text can be added into the appropriate textbox (Figure 5.46). With the image added the page looks like Figure 5.47.

If the left cursor key is pressed once in order to move the cursor to the left of the image, the text can be typed onto the page or imported from a word processor using the Copy and Paste method. However, the desired word wrapping is not obtained by default, and the text would simply move the image down the page (Figure 5.48). In order to get the word

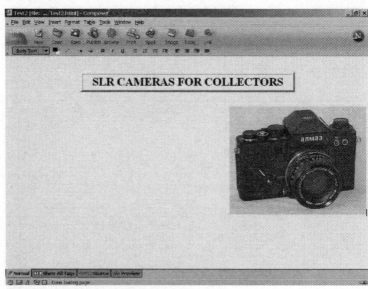

Fig.5.47 An image added to the page

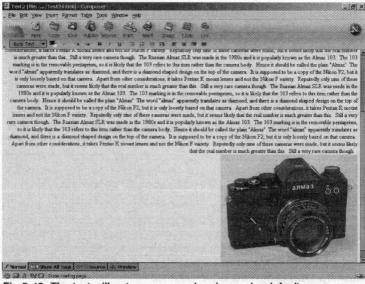

Fig.5.48 The text will not wrap around an image by default

wrapping it is necessary to right-click on the image and then select Image Properties from the pop-up menu that appears. This produces the same window that was used to load the image, but in this case it is the facilities available under the Appearance tab that are required (Figure 5.49). The Wrap to Left option is selected

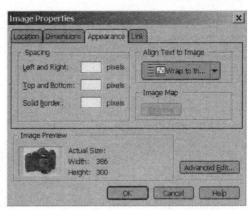

Fig.5.49 The Appearances section of the Image Properties window

in the Align Text to Image menu, and the required wrapping to the left of the image should then be obtained, as in Figure 5.50.

Fig.5.50 The text has correctly wrapped around the image

Fig.5.51 The text wraps too closely around the image

It is possible to add some refinements to the page. The subheading can be selected and changed to one of the smaller sizes of heading text. The rest of the text can be selected and justified by operating the Align Justify button on the toolbar. This gives something like Figure 5.51, which looks better but has a flaw. The text runs right up to the image and, particularly at the left side of the image, practically merges with it. This can be corrected by right-clicking on the image and selecting Image Properties again. In the Appearances section there are two textboxes where figures that control the spacing around the image can be added. Figure 5.52 shows the page with a Left and Right setting of 20 pixels and a Top and Bottom setting of 10 pixels. There is also an option to have a solid border around the image, and in the example of Figure 5.53 the border has a thickness of three pixels.

Dialogue boxes

Having completed a dummy web page it is worthwhile experimenting a little. Netscape Composer does not have facilities for dragging the cell walls of tables, dragging images to the required size and position, or

Fig.5.52 A "no-go zone" has been placed around the image

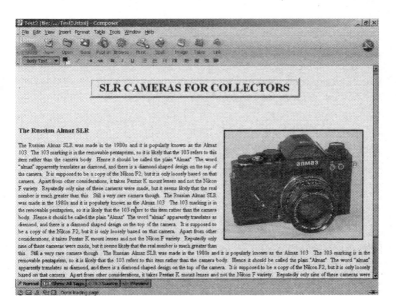

Fig.5.53 A border can be placed around the image

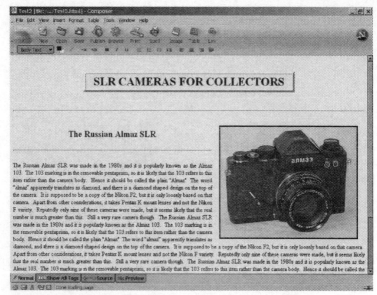

Fig.5.54 The revamped page, complete with horizontal lines

anything of this type. However, there are numerous dialogue boxes that can be used to control all manner of things. In most cases they can be accessed by either right-clicking on an object and selecting the appropriate option from the popup menu, or double-clicking the object to bring up its properties window.

For example, suppose you wish to try a new background colour for a table. Double-clicking the table, other than on any text it contains, will produce the Table Properties window. This permits various parameters to be changed, and it includes a button that produces the colour swatch so that a new background colour can be changed. Double-clicking an image brings up the Image Properties window where it is possible to select a different image, alter the spacing around the image, etc. Horizontal lines can be added by placing the text cursor at the appropriate point on the page and then selecting Horizontal Line from the Insert menu. Double-clicking on the line brings up the Horizontal Line Properties window so that the width, alignment, and height can be edited.

Figure 5.54 shows a revamped version of the page, complete with a couple of horizontal lines, which do not really work that well in this case.

Fig.5.55 The page is displayed very accurately in Netscape Navigator

If you change something and do decide you preferred the original, selecting Undo from the Edit menu will remove the change. It can be reinstated by selecting Redo from the Edit menu. An object can be deleted by right-clicking on it and then selecting Delete from the popup menu. Alternatively, select it and then operate the Delete key.

Netscape Composer has a Preview mode that can be accessed via the button at the bottom of the screen, but the only certain way of checking a page is to view it in a couple of browsers. Figure 5.55 shows the page in Netscape Navigator, and as one would probably expect, it has reproduced the page very accurately. Things are less good in Internet Explorer (Figure 5.56) where the headline has gone slightly awry. Although less than ideal it is just about passable like this. Some experimenting with the table's parameters might affect a cure.

Anchors and links

It is of course possible to add anchors and links using Netscape Communicator. For this example the dummy page has been enlarged

Fig.5.56 *Results are not quite as good using Internet Explorer*

Fig.5.57 *The list added to the page*

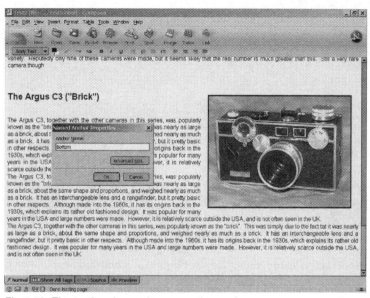

Fig.5.58 The textbox is used to name the anchor

by adding three more sections. An unordered (bulleted) list will be added near the top of the page and used to automatically scroll down to the three lower sections via anchors and links. The list is added by placing the text cursor at the correct point in the document and selecting List from the Format menu. The Bulleted option is then selected from the submenu that appears. A bullet will then appear to the left of the text cursor, and the text for the first item in the list is typed alongside it. Operating the Return key produces another bullet on the next line, the text for the second item in the list is entered, and the Return key is pressed again, and so on until the list is finished. Figure 5.57 shows the page with the list added.

Next an anchor will be added at the bottom of the page to match the link for the last item in the list. The text cursor is placed in the bottom line of the page and then Named Anchor is selected from the Insert menu. This produces a small window where a name for the anchor is added into the textbox (Figure 5.58) and then the OK button is operated. An anchor symbol should then appear in the text to show that the anchor has been added successfully (Figure 5.59).

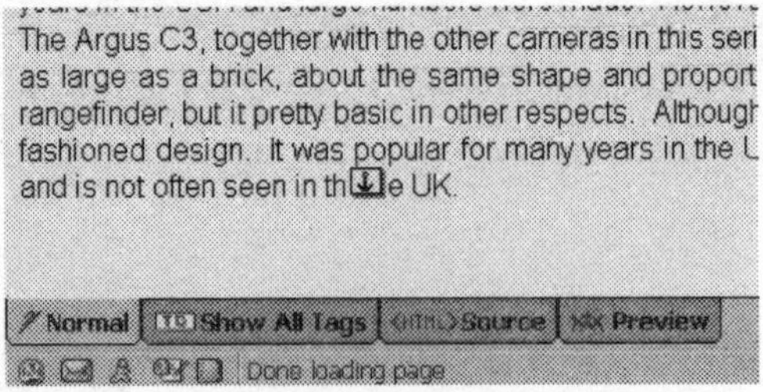

The Argus C3, together with the other cameras in this seri
as large as a brick, about the same shape and proport
rangefinder, but it pretty basic in other respects. Although
fashioned design. It was popular for many years in the U
and is not often seen in the UK.

The link is added to the list by selecting the appropriate piece of text and then choosing Link from the Insert menu. This launches the Link Properties window, and the menu gives a list of the available files and anchors in the site (Figure 5.60).

Fig.5.59 An anchor symbol appears in the text

With the right one selected it is just a matter of operating the OK button. The link text should then change to blue and it will also be underlined, indicating that the link has been added successfully.

This whole procedure is then repeated for the other two list entries that will be used as links. There is no need to add a link to the first entry in the list, since this section of the page is already displayed when the list is on the screen. The list could be repeated at the bottom of the page with

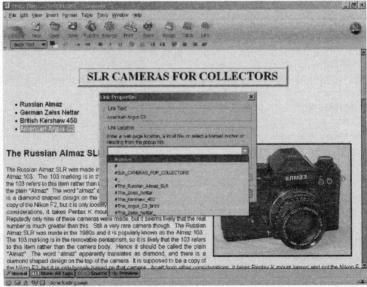

Fig.5.60 The new anchor should appear in the list of files and anchors

Fig.5.61 The links have been added to the list

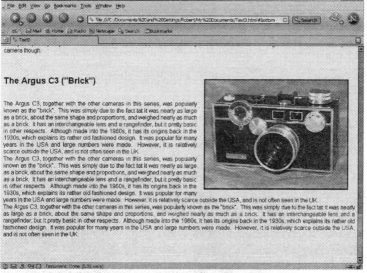

Fig.5.62 The page has correctly scrolled to the bottom

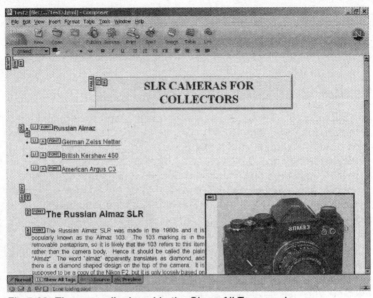

Fig.5.63 The page displayed in the Show All Tags mode

links to the top three sections, but for this example we will keep things simple and settle for a single list. Figure 5.61 shows the completed page in Netscape Navigator, and Figure 5.62 shows the result of activating the bottom link in the list. The page has correctly been scrolled right down to the bottom.

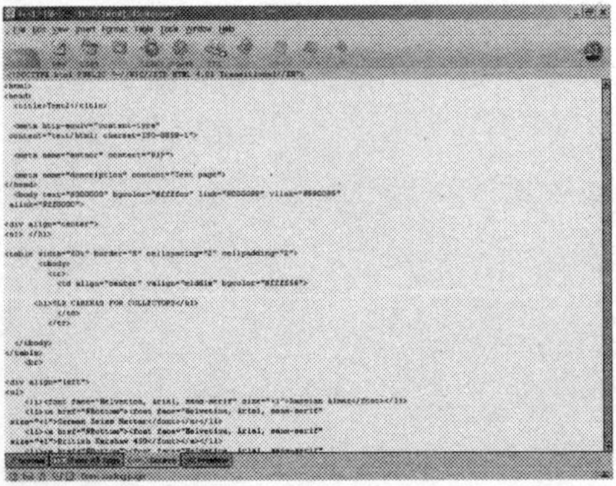

When things are not going as expected with Netscape Composer it can be useful to switch to the Show All Tags mode by operating the button at the bottom of the screen. As its name suggests, this mode shows all the

Fig.5.64 The HTML can be viewed

tags, which appear as yellow boxes containing a short piece of text to identify them (Figure 5.63). Those with a good knowledge of HTML coding can take things a stage further and switch to the HTML mode, which shows the code generated by the program (Figure 5.64).

Fusion

Netscape Composer is a quite a powerful page creation program, and it is certainly capable of producing complex web pages. It is well worth considering if you require a reasonably straightforward means of producing web pages and do not wish to buy a page creation program. It certainly ranks as one of the best free downloads on the Internet. Although Netscape Composer is a WYSIWYG page creation program, its facilities fall well short of those provided by a modern WYSIWYG desktop publishing program. It is not possible to reposition images or blocks of text by dragging them around the screen, or to drag the cell walls of tables to new positions.

There are programs that provide facilities such as these, and which enable pages to be composed in something close to standard desktop publishing fashion. The fact that HTML pages are being produced is, as far as possible, hidden from the user. Netobjects Fusion is about as close as you can get to a desktop publishing program for web pages, and although it was once quite expensive, it has been repositioned at the low-cost end of the market. It was used in chapter two to demonstrate the wizard approach to site construction, but it can be used without the wizard if you wish to "do your own thing". Start by selecting New Site from the File menu, followed by Blank Site from the submenu. A file browser will then appear so that the site can be named and saved to the correct folder. The program then goes into the Site View mode and shows the current layout of the pages in the site.

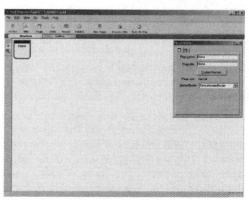

Fig.5.65 Only the homepage is produced by default

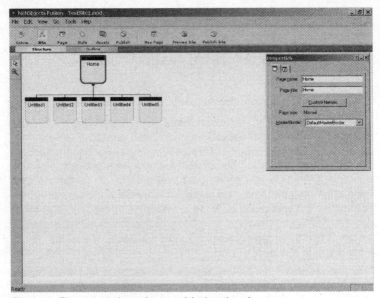

Fig.5.66 Five pages have been added to the site

At this stage the layout is extremely simple, because only the homepage
is produced by default (Figure 5.65). Suppose you need five pages that
will be accessed by way of links from the homepage. Simply operating
the New Page button five times will add the new pages to the site (Figure
5.66). Perhaps one of the pages will need a linked page for additional
material. Start by left-clicking the page that needs the additional page.
This will select it (the selected page is outlined in blue), and it is then just
a matter of operating the New Page button to add the extra page. You
can add as many pages as required by using the same basic method,
working down the chain until all the required pages have been added.
Figure 5.67 shows the site after it has been expanded in this way.

By default the homepage is called Home and the others are called
Untitled1, Untitled2, and so on. The name of a page can be changed by
selecting it and editing the text in the two textboxes in the Properties
window. This is a floating window, but by default it appears near the top
right-hand corner of the screen. Note that its function will change
depending on the mode and tool selected at the time. Each page has
two names, and the one in the Page Title field is the name that appears
in the title bar at the top of the web page when it is viewed using a

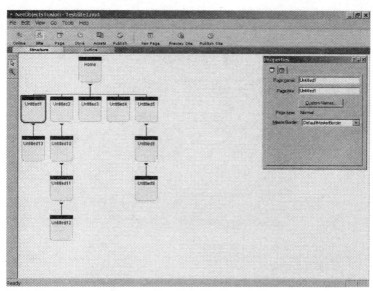

Fig.5.67 More pages are easily added to the existing ones

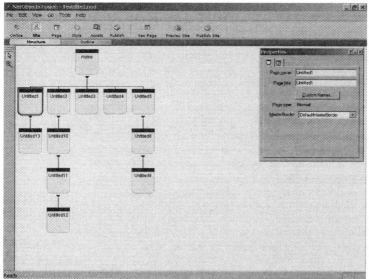

Fig.5.68 The pages have been given meaningful names

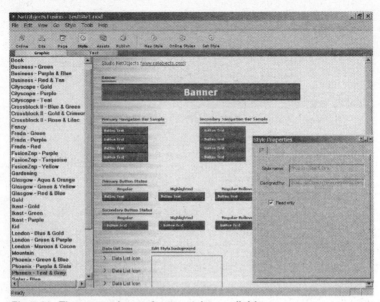

Fig.5.69 There are plenty of page styles available

browser. This name should therefore be something sensible as it will be seen by visitors to your site.

The Page Name field is used internally, and this is the name that will appear in the site map for example. You can simply use the same name for both, but the page title is often quite long. Most users prefer to use shorter names for the page name when a long title is used. The page name is used on navigation buttons, which more or less obliges you to use a short name. Figure 5.68 shows the site with the pages given meaningful names and titles.

Page style

It is advisable to choose the page style before starting to add any content. Operating the Style button in the bar just below the menu bar changes the screen to look something like Figure 6.69. Alternative styles can be selected by left-clicking on their entries in the list down the left-hand side of the screen. The selected style is previewed in the right-hand section of the screen. For this example the Cityscape – Teal style was selected

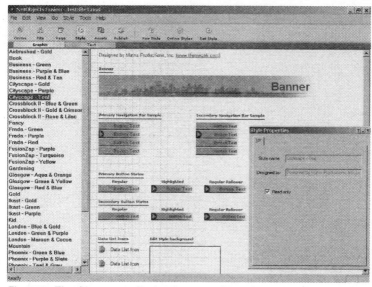

Fig.5.70 The Cityscape - Teal style was selected

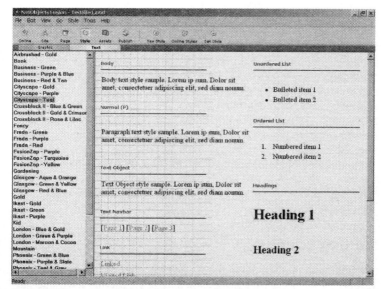

Fig.5.71 The text styles can also be previewed

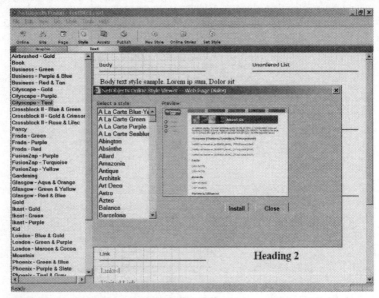

Fig.5.72 Further styles are available online

(Figure 5.70). Note that the text style can be previewed by operating the Text tab that is situated on the left-hand side near the top of the window (Figure 5.71).

The range of built-in styles is quite large, but a further selection can be obtained by operating the Online Styles button (Figure 5.72). Of course, it is only possible to use this facility if your PC has an active Internet connection. In order to use one of the online styles it is just a matter of selecting it from the list and then operating the Install button. After a short delay while it downloads, the selected style will be added to the list in the main Styles window, and it can then be used in the same way as the built-in styles. Actually, once downloaded and installed it becomes a built-in style. The selected style is applied to the site by operating the Set Style button.

Adding content

With the basic structure of the site in place it is time to start adding content to the pages. Operate the site button to return to the site view, and then

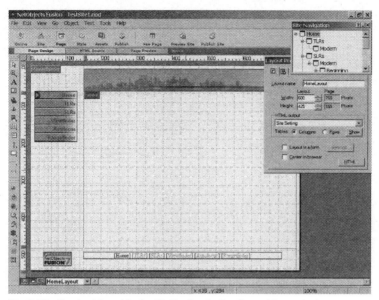

Fig.5.73 Content is added with Fusion in the Page View mode

double-click on the page that you wish to work on. This takes Fusion into the Page View mode for that page (Figure 5.73). The page has a standard frames layout with a banner at the top, a navigation frame on the left, the content frame to the right, and a navigation bar at the bottom. The Fusion 7 logo also appears here, but it can be removed by selecting it and operating the Delete key. The frames at the top, left, and bottom form the master border, and they are present on every page in the site. Anything on them is also present on every page, so removing the Fusion logo on one page removes it from every page in the site.

Apart from removing the logo, few, if any, changes are made to the master border. The content frame is the one where most of your efforts will be concentrated. Text can be added to the content frame by selecting the Text tool from the toolbar situated on the left-hand side of the screen. Its button is the one marked with a letter "A". A box for the text is automatically generated when you left-click in the content frame, and this box will expand to accommodate the text as more is added. The usual handles on the bounding box enable the size and shape of the box to be controlled manually.

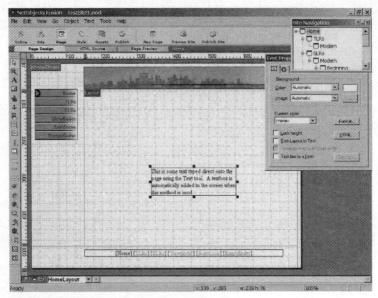

Fig.5.74 Some text added to the page

It is possible to drag the box anywhere within the content frame. First left-click somewhere outside the box to deselect it, and then left-click within the box to select it again. It can then be moved by dragging anywhere within the box. Double-click within the box to make the text cursor appear so that more text can be added. Figure 5.74 shows some text added to the page. Of course, text can also be added by preparing it in a word processor and transferring it to the content frame using the copy and paste method.

When the text cursor is present, the Properties window goes into the Text Properties mode and it then provides the usual features for aligning text, changing its size and style, and so on. This all works in standard word processor fashion and formatting the text is therefore very quick and simple. A fully justified alignment option is available, together with a good range of text sizes. A different version of the Text Properties window is produced when the textbox is selected. Amongst other things, this permits the background colour to be changed (Figure 5.75) or a background image to be added.

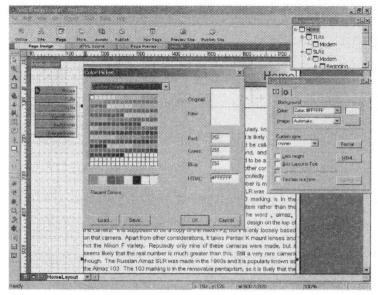

Fig.5.75 The background colour can be changed or an image added

Adding images

Adding images using Fusion is very simple and straightforward. First select the Picture tool by operating the appropriate button in the toolbar (the one beneath the Text tool button). Left-click at the point where the image is to be added, and a file browser will then appear (Figure 5.76) so that the image can be selected. Operate the Open button to add the selected image to the page (Figure 5.77). If you wish to have Alt text for the image it is typed into the Alt Tag textbox in the Picture Properties window.

The image has been added to the page but the overall result is not very good. The text has not wrapped around the image and there is a blank area to its right. This can be corrected by selecting the correct alignment option for the image. Operate the alignment tab (the third one from the left) and then select the appropriate option, which in this case is Left Wrap. The text then flows around the image in the desired fashion (Figure 5.78). If you change your mind and would prefer the picture on the right, simply select the Right Wrap option and the page will change accordingly (Figure 5.79).

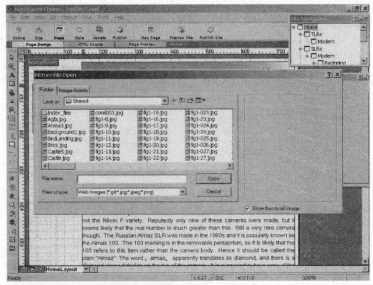

Fig.5.76 The file browser used for adding images

Fig.5.77 The image added into the text

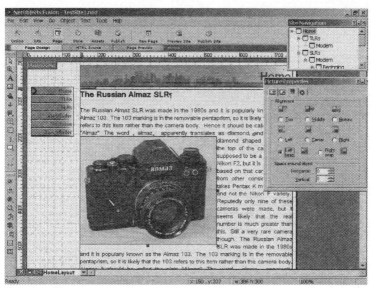

Fig.5.78 The page with the Left Wrap option selected

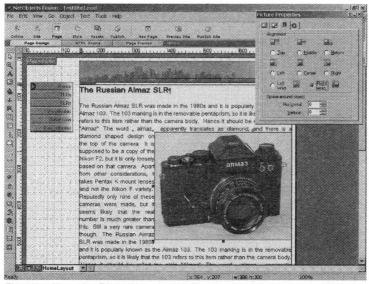

Fig.5.79 Here the Right Wrap option has been chosen

Fig.5.80 A blank area can be placed around the image

Although the text is now wrapping around the image correctly, there is the usual problem of it getting too close to the image in places. Adding suitable values into the Space Around textboxes in the Picture Properties window will move the text out from the image. Figure 5.80 shows the example page with the horizontal and vertical spacing values both set at 10 pixels. With the Normal mode set in the first page of the Picture Properties window it is not possible to make the image larger than its natural size. Dragging the bounding box to a smaller size results in the image being cropped (Figure 5.81).

Switching to the Stretch mode enables the image to be freely changed in size (Figure 5.82), including enlargement. Hold down the Control key while resizing an image if you wish to avoid changing its aspect ratio. Bear in mind that significant enlargement of an image can give rather rough looking results. Enlarging an image by a small amount to make it fit into the layout more neatly is fine, but anything beyond this is questionable.

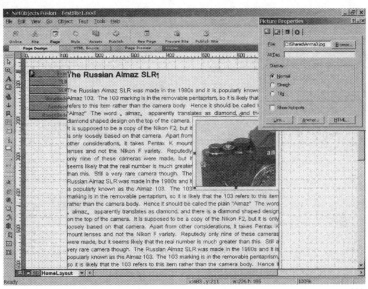

Fig.5.81 A smaller bounding box crops the image

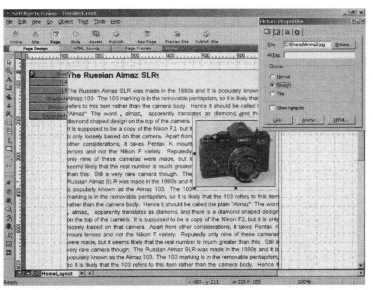

Fig.5.82 The Stretch mode enables the image to be resized

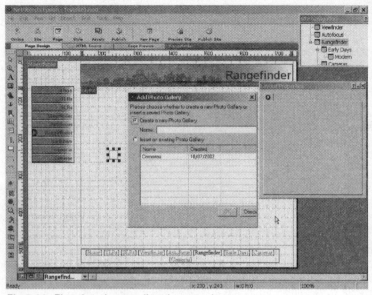

Fig.5.83 First the photo gallery is named

Photo gallery

Fusion has a built-in facility for making photo gallery pages. Start by using the Site View facility or the Site Navigation window to select the correct page in the site. Next the Photo Gallery tool is selected from the toolbar, and its button is the eighth one up. Left-click somewhere in the content frame and then add a name for the gallery in the small window that appears (Figure 5.83). Operate the OK button and a much larger window will then appear (Figure 5.84). This is a form of file browser, and the required files are selected and loaded one by one. The buttons enable files in the list to be selected and moved up or down, or they can be dragged to a new position, so it is easy to change the order. A title and a caption can optionally be added via the textboxes in the upper right-hand section of the window.

The default values should give good results, but you may like to operate the Thumbnail tab and select a different style for the thumbnail page (Figure 5.85). Operating the Photo Page tab enables the layout for the photo page to be altered (Figure 5.86). Left-click the Done button when

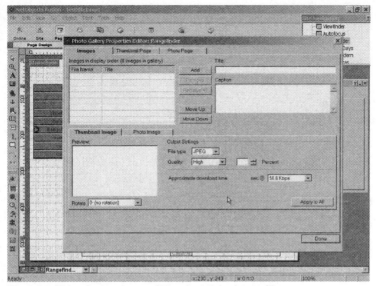

Fig.5.84 This window is used to select the picture files

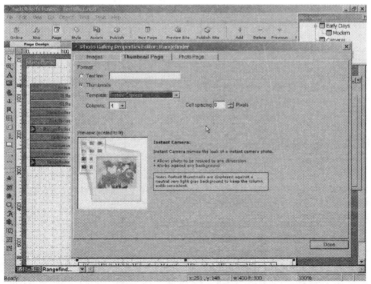

Fig.5.85 Alternative styles are available for the thumbnail page

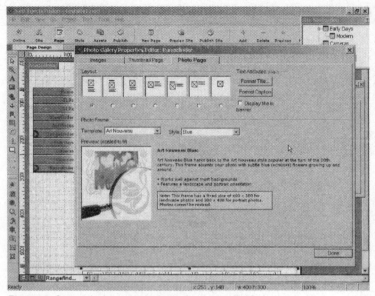

Fig.5.86 Several photo page layouts are available

you have finished, and the content page should contain the thumbnail views of the photographs (Figure 5.87).

Testing

The site can be tested by operating the Preview Site button, which launches the default browser and loads the current page. Figure 5.88 shows the thumbnail page previewed in Internet Explorer, and everything appears as it should be. Left-clicking on a thumbnail image results in the photo page and the appropriate photograph appearing, complete with title and caption (Figure 5.89). The navigation frame is fully operational, and operating the Home button results in the final version of the dummy homepage appearing (Figure 5.90).

The current page can be previewed by operating the Page Preview tab, and quite accurate results are obtained (Figure 5.91). Note though, that this facility is strictly for previewing the current page, and that neither the navigation buttons nor any links function in this mode. In order to test links it is necessary to preview the site in a browser. Operating the HTML

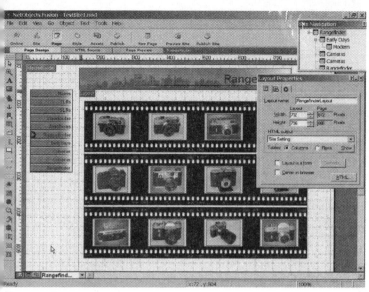

Fig.5.87 The completed thumbnail page

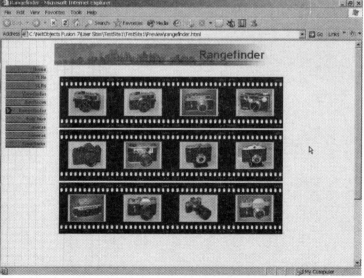

Fig.5.88 The thumbnail page in the Preview Site mode

Fig.5.89 The correct photo page has been displayed

Fig.5.90 Operating the Home button has brought up the homepage

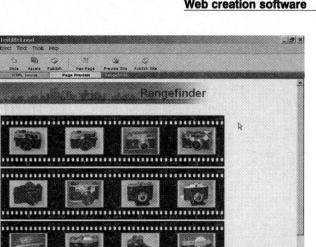

Fig.5.91 The thumbnail page in the Page Preview mode

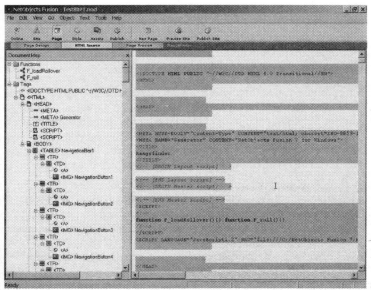

Fig.5.92 The HTML code can be viewed

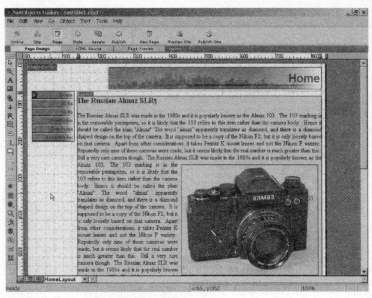

Fig.5.93 The original version of the page

tab enables the HTML code to be viewed (Figure 5.92), but with a program like Fusion you do not really need any knowledge of HTML.

Fusion does not give quite the same freedom as a good desktop publishing program, but using it to lay out web pages it still quite easy. Suppose that you wished alter the dummy homepage (Figure 5.93) by moving the camera photograph slightly higher up the page. With most desktop publishing programs you could simply drag the photograph higher and the text would automatically reformat around it. Changing the size of the photograph will produce automatic reformatting of the text, but it can not be dragged to a new position.

The image is inserted in the text at a certain point, and this point is indicated by a blue marker. It is at the beginning of the word "Russian" in the line above the photograph. The photograph can be moved by selecting it, choosing Cut from the Edit menu, positioning the text cursor further up the page, and then selecting Paste from the Edit menu (Figure 5.94). It is a relatively cumbersome method, but it is a limitation of HTML coding, which treats images a bit like outsize text characters. It is possible to move pictures around the screen and place them anywhere you like if

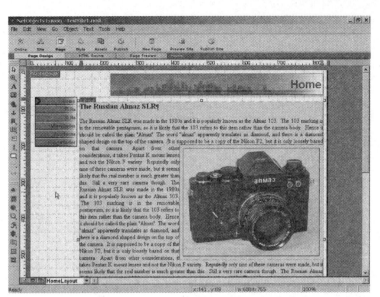

Fig.5.94 Cut and Paste have been used to move the image

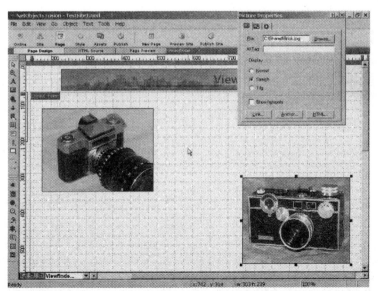

Fig.5.95 Images outside a textbox can be place anywhere on the page

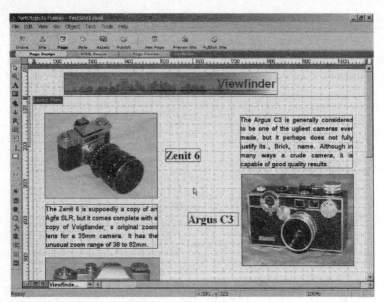

Fig.5.96 Text can be added as and where required

they are not within a textbox, as in Figure 5.95. However, it is not possible to then flow text around the images. The text just flows straight over the images. Text can be placed in textboxes though, and these can be positioned wherever you like using the dragging method (Figure 5.96).

Fusion is designed for professionals, but it is straightforward to use and is well suited to beginners as well. It is a program that you are unlikely to outgrow.   A 30-day trial version can be downloaded from www.netobjects.com, and it is well worthwhile downloading and experimenting with this program. By producing one or two dummy sites you will soon learn a great deal about producing web pages and sites.

FrontPage

Microsoft's FrontPage is worthy of mention even though it costs slightly too much to be considered a budget site creation program. It is included with some versions of Microsoft's Office suite of programs. In general it is only included with the more upmarket versions of Office, but it has occasionally been included with the less expensive versions as a special

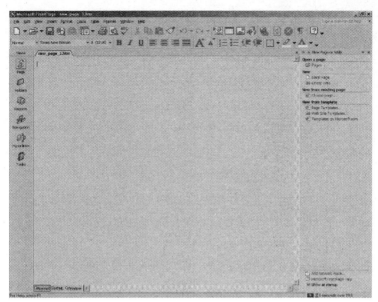

Figh.5.97 FrontPage has the standard Office look

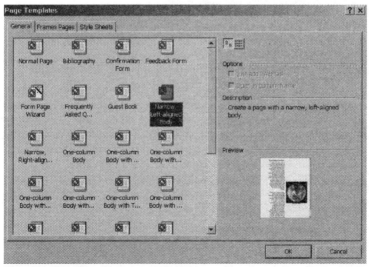

Fig.5.98 The Page Templates window

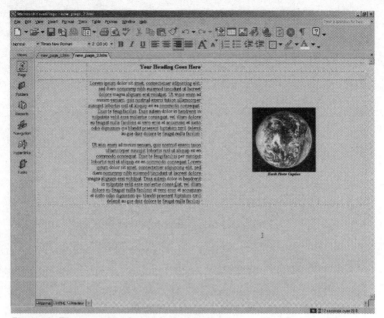

*Fig.5.99 The template is loaded with dummy content that must be
replaced with your own material*

promotion. Anyway, if you have Office installed on your PC it is worth
checking to see if FrontPage has been installed as part of this suite of
programs. There is probably no point in bothering with any other web
creation software if you already have FrontPage.

It offers a full range of features including some quite advanced ones.
Note though, that some of the clever features will only work if your site is
hosted on a server that supports FrontPage extensions. There may be
an additional fee for this facility, but the popularity of FrontPage is such
that web space providers are unlikely to charge much for including a
facility to use its extensions. Of course, the FrontPage extensions are
only needed for sites that use the advanced features, such as those that
give interactivity with users of the site. The extensions are not needed
for a "no frills" site.

On launching FrontPage it has the usual Office look (Figure 5.97), and it
looks remarkably similar to Word. There are various ways of building a
page, and one is to use a template. Operating the Page Templates link

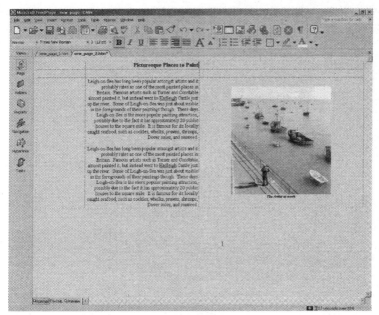

Fig.5.100 The dummy content is easily replaced

in the right-hand panel produces the Templates window (Figure 5.98). A thumbnail view of the selected template is shown in the Preview panel, so it is easy to go through them and choose the one that best fits your requirements. With the template loaded (Figure 5.99) it is then a matter of going through the usual process of replacing the existing content with the real thing (Figure 5.100).

Web site templates

Alternatively, there is the option of using a site template. Operating the site template link produces the Web Site Templates window (Figure 5.101), where the most apt template is selected. This brings up the initial window of the Web Site Template Wizard (Figure 5.102), and in subsequent pages the usual wizard style windows appear, and the required parameters are selected.

Figure 5.103 shows an example screen produced by the Web Site Templates Wizard. When the process is complete the program goes

5 Web creation software

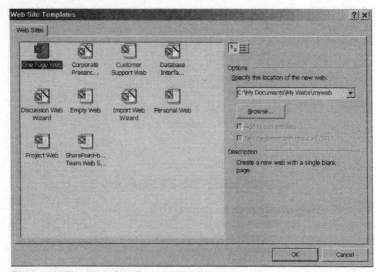

Fig.5.101 The Web Site Templates window

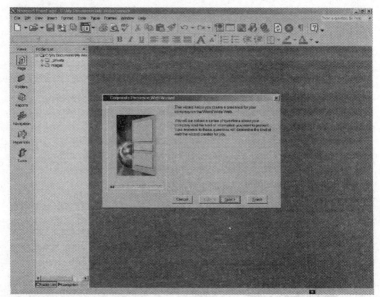

Fig.5.102 The opening page of the Web Site Wizard

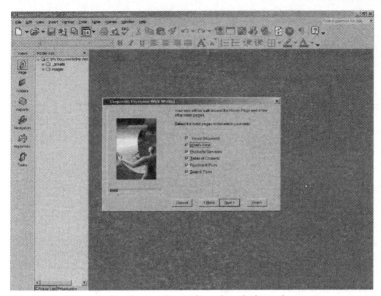

Fig.5.103 This window is used to select the site's main pages

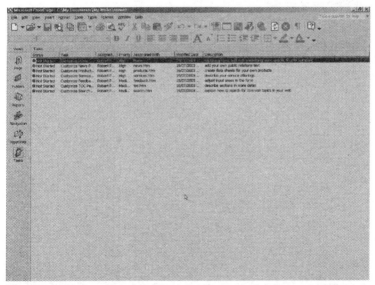

Fig.5.104 The program defaults to the Tasks mode after completion

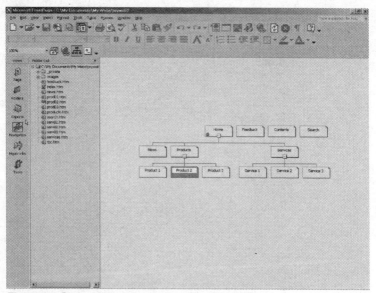

Fig.5.105 Site mode shows a diagram of the site

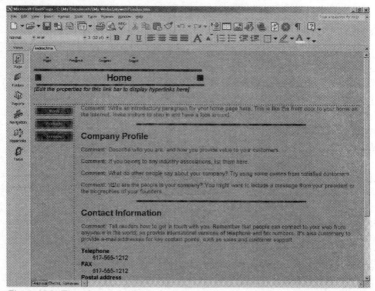

Fig.5.106 The dummy pages indicate the type of content required

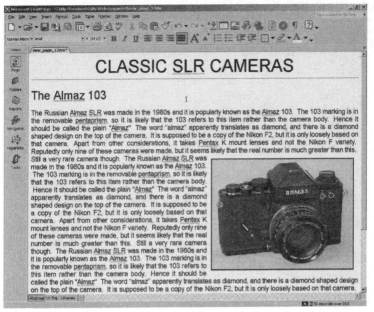

Fig.5.107 FrontPage can also be used to produce single web pages

into the Tasks mode by default (Figure 5.104), and initially this simply shows that none of the tasks have been started. Operating the Navigation button produces a site map (Figure 5.105), and double-clicking on one of the pages in the diagram opens the corresponding page (Figure 5.106). As usual, the dummy content is then replaced with the proper content for that page.

FrontPage is a very sophisticated program, but it can be used to produce a single page if that is all you need. Figure 5.107 shows the FrontPage version of the cameras dummy page, and it was produced in much the same way as before. The text was added to the page first, with the image then being inserted into the text. Next the correct wrap style was selected, and so on. FrontPage is perhaps not as easy to use as Fusion and some other web creation programs, but it is worth persevering with it. Once you have gained some experience with FrontPage it can be used to produce most types of web site quite quickly and efficiently.

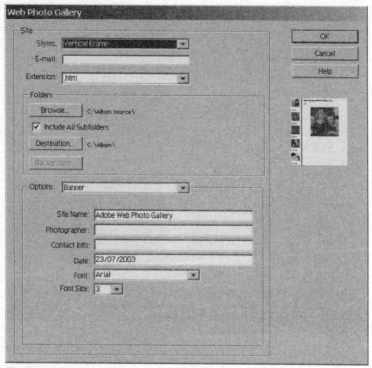

Fig.5.108 There is a choice of several photo album styles

Photo albums

Many graphics programs can produce HTML pages, but they do not represent a good choice for producing most types of web page. One exception is when you need to produce a photo album. There are facilities for producing photo albums built into many web page creation programs, so using a graphics program is not the only option. It is often the easiest way of handling things though. Photoshop Elements 2 has one of the best photo album facilities, and it makes the task about as easy as it possibly could be.

The first task is to select Create Photo Web Gallery from the File menu, and this launches the Web Photo Gallery window (Figure 5.108). The Style menu at the top of the window provides a choice of 15 page layouts. The Folders section of the window permits the source and destination

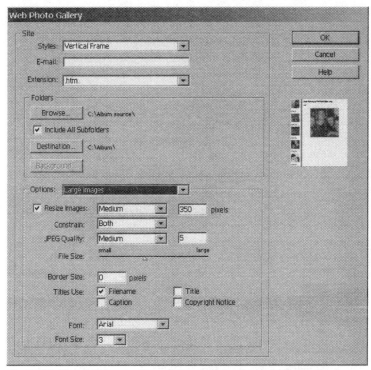

Fig.5.109 The bottom section of the window changes to suit the parameter selected from the Options menu

folders to be selected. The image files for the album must be placed in a folder prior to using the photo gallery facility. Include nothing other than the image files in this folder. An empty file to take the photo gallery should also have been produced previously, or it can be made by operating the Destination button and then using the Make Directory button.

The lower part of the window changes to suit the parameter selected in the Options menu. Fig.5.109 shows the window with the Large Images option selected. It is worth spending a little time going through the various options and customising the album to best suit your requirements. Operate the OK button when everything has been set up to your satisfaction. Photoshop Elements will then go through the images one by one, processing them as necessary, and building the photo album.

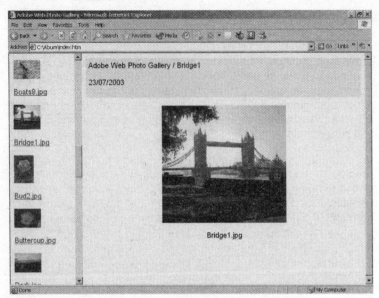

Fig.5.110 The completed album viewed in Internet Explorer

The completed album will be shown in the default web browser (Figure 5.110). By default the main HTML page will be called index.htm, so it will act as the homepage if it is uploaded to a server. Note that the album will only work properly if all the support files and folders are uploaded as well. Rename index.htm if you wish to use the album as part of a larger site.

Points to remember

These days practically any text or graphics program can be used to produce HTML pages, but many of these programs are not well suited to producing web pages and sites. If you have programs that can produce HTML pages there is nothing to lose by trying to use them to produce some web pages. It is better to try other options if the programs prove to be ill suited to the task.

Word, the ever popular word processor program, can easily handle the production of text-only web pages, as can most up-to-date word processors. In fact Word can handle quite complex web pages and even complete web sites. It is certainly worth trying it for web site creation if you already have a copy installed on your PC.

There are plenty of free programs that can be used to produce web pages, but most of them require a good knowledge of HTML coding. Few are in the WYSIWYG category. Netscape Composer is part of the Netscape suite of programs, and it provides a relatively easy means of producing web pages, complete with a WYSIWYG display. It is available as a free download, so it costs little or nothing to try.

In general, web creation programs do not provide the same sort of freedom as desktop publishing programs. This is due to the fact that HTML coding imposes some limitations on page layouts. Things that are possible with an upmarket desktop publishing program will not necessarily convert well into HTML code.

A powerful, full-featured, web site creation program does not have to cost hundreds of pounds. Fusion for example, costs well under a hundred pounds and has enough features for professional use. It is also easy for beginners to use though, and it is about as close as you can currently get to a desktop publishing program for producing web pages.

FrontPage is included with some versions of Microsoft's Office suite. It is not as easy to use as some web creation programs, but it is capable of producing anything from simple one-page sites to sophisticated multi-page types. If you already have FrontPage on your PC it is worth taking some time to learn how to use it.

Many programs that can produce web sites have templates and (or) wizards that can help you produce the "bare bones" of a site. With the basic site created it is then a matter of filling the pages with the real content, and perhaps doing some customisation. The links between pages and overall structure of the site are handled by the wizard or template.

The templates and wizards of many programs that can produce web pages include at least one specifically for producing photo albums. This usually offers a very quick and easy way of producing professional looking albums.

Uploading and promotion

Integral upload

Having built your new web site there is the minor matter of uploading it to the server. The traditional method is to use an FTP program to upload all the files, but it is increasingly common for web creation programs to have a built-in facility for uploading pages or even complete sites. The facilities provided vary considerably from one program to another. Netscape Composer has one of the more simple forms of built-in uploading facility, but it is still useful when initially publishing a site.

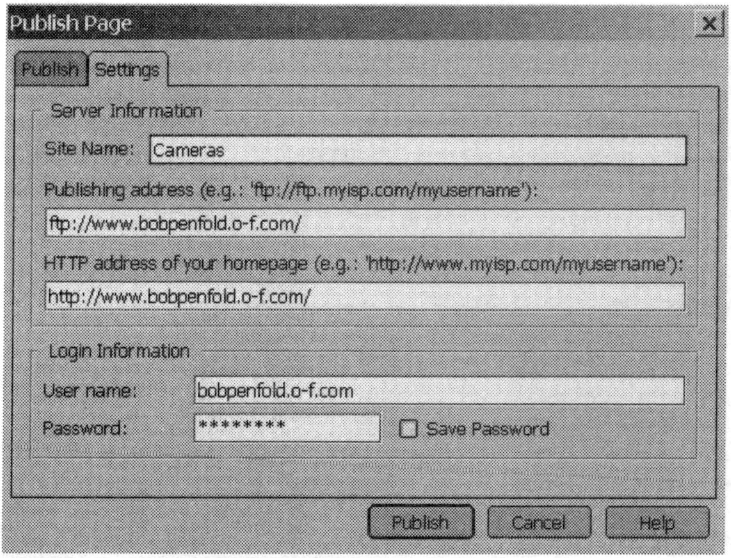

Fig.6.1 The Publish Page window of Netscape Composer

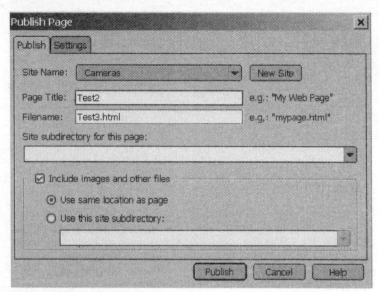

Fig.6.2 *Make sure the Include images and other files checkbox is ticked*

In order to upload a page it is first loaded into Composer. Then the Publish option is selected from the File menu, which produces the window shown in Figure 6.1. Here a name for the site is added in the textbox at the top, and the other fields are used to add the password and other information provided by your web host during the signup process. Composer needs this information to find the correct server and gain access to it. Even one minor error here will probably prevent the files from being uploaded. Note that much or all of this information is case sensitive, so be careful to enter it in exactly as provided by the web host.

With the information entered and checked, operate the Publish tab to bring up the new version of the window shown in Figure 6.2. Here the default settings should suffice, but make sure that the "Include images and other files" radio button is active. If it is not, the HTML file will be uploaded but any images or other support files will not. Operating the Publish button starts the uploading process. A window that shows how things are progressing will open (Figure 6.3), and this will automatically close once the process has been completed. Bear in mind that most Internet connections upload more slowly than they download. A 56k connection only uploads at 33k for example, and a 512k ADSL connection

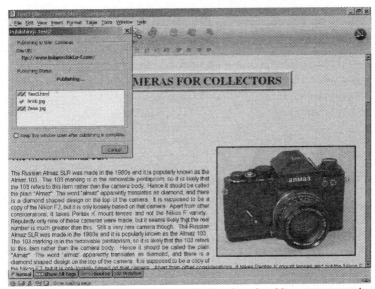

Fig.6.3 A small window shows how far the download has progressed

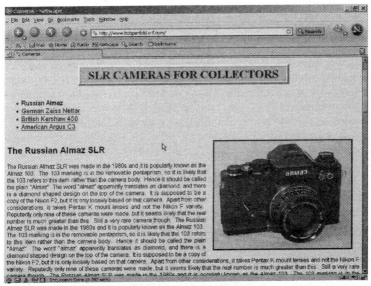

Fig.6.4 The site has been successfully uploaded

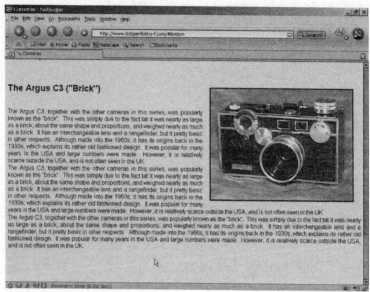

Fig.6.5 *The page has correctly scrolled to the bottom*

uploads at a more modest 256k. It can take quite a while to upload large sites with a 56/33k Internet connection.

The example site uploaded successfully, but trying to access the site produced a message stating that there was no index page at that address. The reason for this is simple: I had made the classic mistake of forgetting to rename the page as "index.html". A homepage can be called anything you like when it is on your PC, but it will only work on the Internet if it is called "index.html" or "index.htm". Saving the page under the correct name and then repeating the upload process rectified the problem, and the page was found at the appropriate web address (Figure 6.4). Operating the bottom link in the list duly scrolled the page down to the final section (Figure 6.5).

Fusion also has a publishing facility, and it is accessed by first opening the site in Fusion and then operating the Publish Site button. This produces the small window of Figure 6.6, and by default the site will be published locally. In other words, it will be published onto the hard disc of the PC. Fusion does not store sites as HTML pages together with support files and folders. Instead, it saves them in its own format. If you

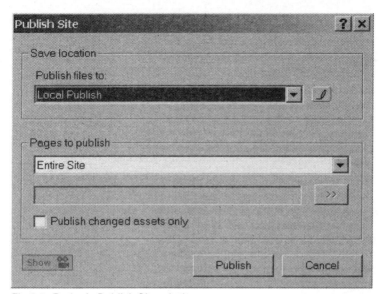

Fig.6.6 Fusion's Publish Site window

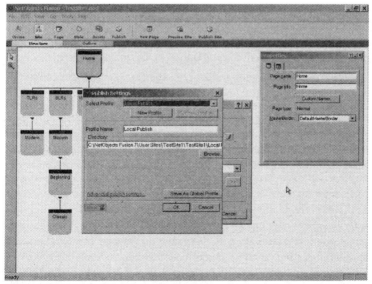

Fig.6.7 Here a new profile is produced

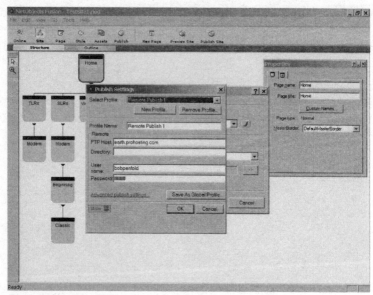

Fig.6.8 Add the information provided by your web host

need to upload the site using an FTP program it is necessary to publish the site to a folder on the hard disc drive first. This produces a site in conventional form that can be uploaded to the server in the normal way.

The alternative is to use the built-in publishing facility that will convert the site into a conventional structure and upload it to the server. In order to do this it is necessary to first operate the button that has the pen icon. This produces the window of Figure 6.7, and here the New Profile button is operated. A tiny window will pop-up, offering the choice of producing a remote profile or a local one, and in this case it is obviously a remote type that is being produced. The window of Figure 6.8 then appears, and it is just a matter of adding the information supplied by your web host. Operate the OK button when you have finished and then operate the Publish button back at the Publish Site window.

A small window will show how well or otherwise the upload process is progressing (Figure 6.9), and eventually a message should appear to indicate that the process has been completed. It is then a matter of checking that the site is indeed present on the Internet, and the homepage of the dummy site was found to be present and correct (Figure 6.10).

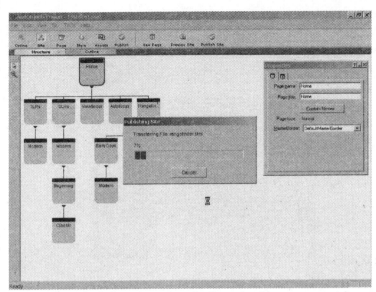

Fig.6.9 A small window shows how far the upload has progressed

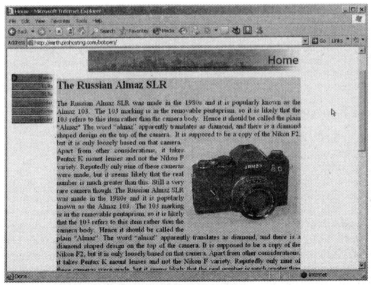

Fig.6.10 The homepage is present and correct

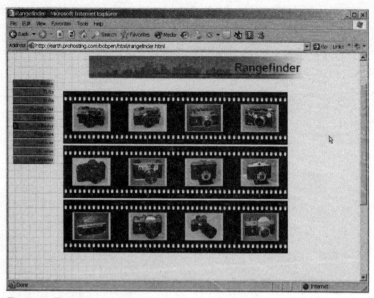

Fig.6.11 The link to the thumbnail page has worked correctly

The dummy site is largely empty, but operating the appropriate navigation button produced the thumbnail page of the photo gallery (Figure 6.11), and left-clicking one of the thumbnails duly produced the correct image (Figure 6.12).

FTP program

Most built-in upload facilities enable the site to be updated, with a new version being uploaded. Any new pages are then added to the site, and new pages will overwrite old ones. Few web creation programs have a built-in facility that genuinely rivals a separate FTP program, so this is the route that you will probably have to take in order to gain full control over your site once it has been uploaded. There are numerous FTP programs available and they mostly have quite low prices. The one that will be used in these examples is WS_FTP LE, which is free for non-corporate users. It can be downloaded from the usual software sources such as www.download.com.

Fig.6.12 The photo album is working as it should

A configuration window pops up when the program is first run (Figure 6.13). A name for the new configuration is typed into the menu textbox at the top of the window, and this could be the name of the web host for example. You can select the host type from the menu, but the automatic option should work well enough. There is no need to add anything in

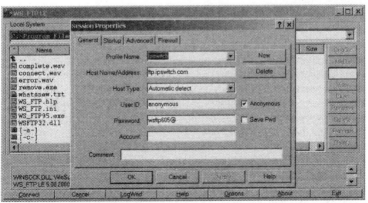

Fig.6.13 A configuration window appears when the program is run

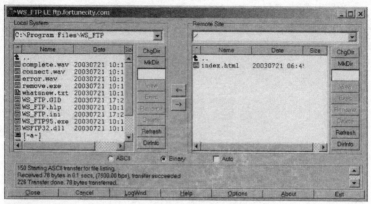

Fig.6.14 There is only one file in the site at this stage

the Account or Comment textboxes. The other three fields are for the information provided by the web space provider, such as the password. Operate the Apply and OK buttons when all the information has been added.

The program should then connect to the web host and the right-hand panel will show the files present in the site (Figure 6.14). Initially it will either be empty or there will be an index file supplied by the web host. This is usually a simple page which explains that the site for that address

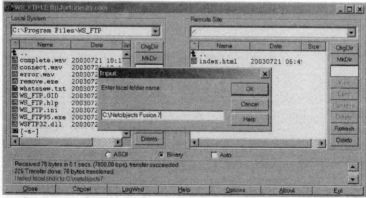

Fig.6.15 Enter the path to the root folder of the site

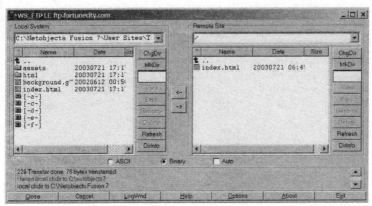

Fig.6.16 The left-hand panel shows the files of the local site

has not been uploaded yet. The index file in your site will overwrite any existing one in due course. The left-hand section of the window shows the files and folders in the default directory. In order to upload your site it is necessary to operate the ChgDir (change directory) button and type

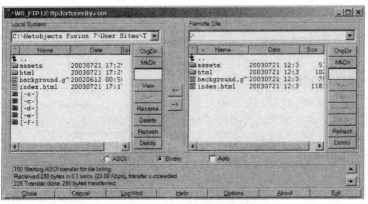

Fig.6.17 The files have been successfully uploaded

the path to the appropriate folder into the textbox that appears (Figure 6.15). The left-hand section of the window will then show the files and folders that must be uploaded.

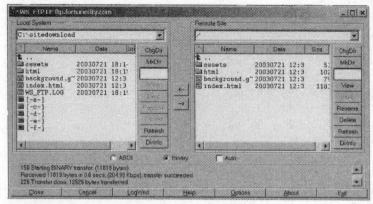

Fig.6.18 Sites can be downloaded as well as uploaded

Next it is a matter of selecting the files and folders that are to be uploaded. This can be achieved by pressing the Control key and left-clicking on each entry that you wish to select. Obviously all the files and folders have to be selected when initially uploading a site. The selected files are uploaded by operating the button between the two panels that has the arrow pointing to the right. A window asking if you wish to go ahead and upload the files will probably appear, and the upload will proceed if the Yes button is operated. The left and right panels should show the same files and folders once the uploading has been completed (Figure 6.17).

File management

With an FTP program it is possible to do more than upload files to the server. Suppose that your hard disc drive fails and the files for your site are lost. The files on the server then constitute the only copy of the site. Using FTP it is just as easy to download files as it is to upload them. In Figure 6.18 the MkDir (make directory) button has been used to make a new directory on the hard disc, and then the ChgDir button has been used to make this the current directory on the local system. The button with the arrow pointing to the left was then operated, and the files on the remote site were downloaded to the new directory.

Using an FTP program it is possible to make changes to the files on the remote site. In Figure 6.19 the program has been connected to the site that was uploaded from Netscape Composer. The original homepage

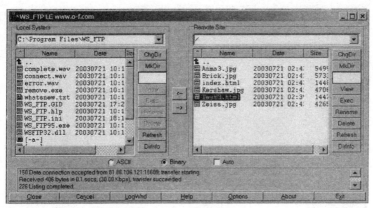

Fig.6.19 The highlighted file is superfluous

file (Test3.html) is listed, as is the version with the correct name (index.html). Of course, only the index.html file is required, and the original file with the wrong name is superfluous. The unwanted file is easily deleted, and it is just a matter of selecting it and then operating the Delete button. Figure 6.20 shows that the file was successfully removed. Using an FTP program it would not have been necessary to upload the renamed version of the file. The original file could have been selected and then renamed by operating the Rename button and typing the correct name into the popup textbox.

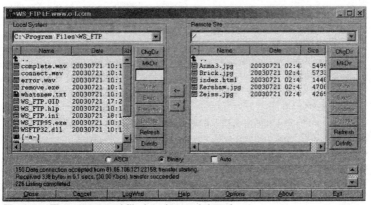

Fig.6.20 The unwanted file has been deleted

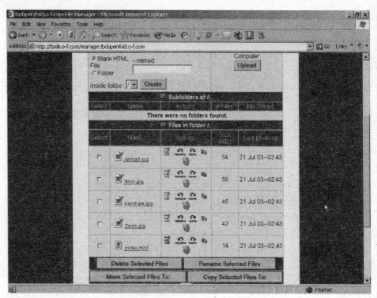

Fig.6.21 An HTML based browser upload facility

Browser upload

Many web hosts have a so-called browser upload facility. A browser
does not have a built-in ability to upload files, and what actually happens
is that an applet or a "clever" HTML page is downloaded to your PC and
then used to upload files. The Geocities FileManager facility described
in chapter three is a form of browser upload facility. Figures 6.21 and
6.22 respectively show the HTML and JavaScript versions of the
www.o-f.com file managers. These provide the usual facilities for deleting
files, renaming them, and so on. Figure 6.23 shows the upload facility of
the JavaScript applet, and this is very similar in operation to the equivalent
Geocities facility.

Where built-in file handling facilities are available they often represent
the easiest way of dealing with files. Initially though, it is often easier to
upload sites using the integral facilities of the site creation program. FTP
or browser based file handling can then be used to help keep things up
to date. Most web hosts have some additional facilities such as site
statistics (Figure 6.24), so it is worthwhile checking to see what is on
offer.

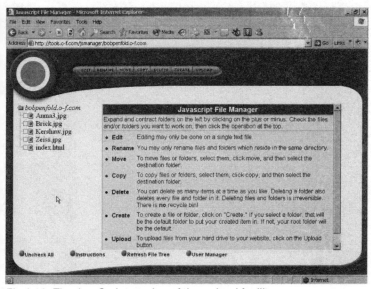

Fig.6.22 The JavaScript version of the upload facility

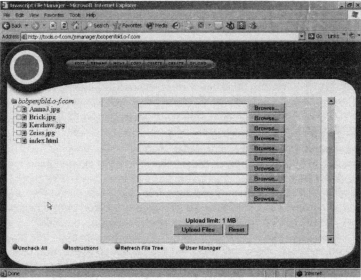

Fig.6.23 This window is used to select the files to be uploaded

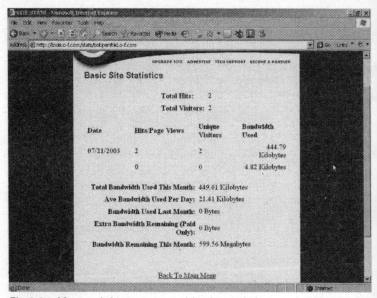

Fig.6.24 Most web hosts can provide site statistics

Fault-finding

Every site should be thoroughly tested before it is uploaded to the server. It should be tested using at least two browsers (Internet Explorer and Netscape Navigator) and preferably at a range of screen resolutions with each browser. Having done this and ascertained that it looks reasonable in each case, and that everything works, surely the uploaded site has to work properly? Unfortunately, it is not quite as simple as that. Things can and sometimes do go wrong when a site is uploaded.

Probably the most common problem is that of the missing image, or possibly some other form of media file. The most likely reason for a media file failing to work is that it is simply not there. Use an FTP program or the web host's file manager program to check that all the files were actually uploaded to your site. Some web site creation programs insist that all the files for the site are in a certain folder on your PC, or in its structure of subfolders. In the case of Fusion for example, the site is stored in its own file format and then it is published to the hard disc or direct to the server. Either way, all the files are placed in one neat folder structure and there is little chance of anything going missing.

With many page and site creation programs it is up to you to ensure that all the files are grouped together and that none are missed out when the site is uploaded. What often goes wrong is that some of the files are stored in general directories used for images, sound files, or whatever, and not with the other site files. These files tend to get overlooked when the site is uploaded, and it therefore fails to work properly. The best way of avoiding this problem is to have images and other media files stored in their own folder within the site's folder structure. If you do not wish to move the media files to the site folders, then use copies of these files in the site. In fact it is probably best to use copies of files in the site anyway.

In order to correct this type of problem it is necessary to move or copy the troublesome files into the site's file structure, and then redo the links to these files. It is then a matter of uploading the corrected version of the site, or any files that have been added or changed. This can be very time consuming and it can be tricky to get everything working properly, so it is better to avoid this type of problem if at all possible.

Relativity

Ideally, when testing a site you should not use the computer that was used to generate the site. Occasionally there can be a problem with an image or other file that fails to make an appearance when someone else accesses the site, but everything seems fine when you test it using the PC used to construct the site. This may seem to be impossible, but there is usually a simple explanation. As pointed out in a previous chapter, links to pages in other sites are absolute. In other words, the full URL of the page has to be specified. These are external links. Internal links to images, other pages in the same site, etc., are relative to either the root folder of the site or to the page containing the link. Using relative links ensures that they still work properly when the site is uploaded to a server, and that they will work with the site on any server.

There will be a problem if you accidentally select the external link option when linking to an internal file. However, the site will still work when it is tested on your PC. The link will be to a file and folder on your PC, such as:

C:\myimages\photos\bigben.jpg

When you are testing the site the browser will look for this file and location on the hard disc drive and it will find it. Accordingly, the page will work properly. When anyone else tries the same link their browser looks in the same location on the hard disc of their PC, but it will not find the file or even that location. The page therefore fails to work properly. The solution is to edit the link by replacing it with one of the correct type, and then upload the page again.

Another common cause of missing images and similar problems is that some of the files have been moved. It is advisable not to mess around with the file structure at all, but any files that are already in use should definitely not be changed. Moving files changes their relative positions in the file structure, and relative links that involve them do not work any more. Some programs can automatically repair broken links when files are moved or renamed, but it is better to play safe and simply leave everything in its original folder.

Missing homepage

Another common problem is that of the missing homepage. Some web site creation programs will automatically produce a homepage with the correct index.html or index.htm name, and will resist attempts to change the name. With many programs you can call the pages whatever you like, and no page called index.html will be produced by default. The site should actually work without an index page, but only by using the full URL in the browser's address bar. It is much better to have the homepage called index.html or inde.htm so that the basic web address can be used to access the site.

Note that in order to be certain that the index page can be accessed properly it is necessary to have the name entirely in lower case letters. Windows does not have case sensitive filenames, but many servers run under UNIX or Linux where the names are case sensitive. Names such as Index.html and INDEX.HTML are unlikely to give the desired result.

Missing FrontPage

If you use FrontPage to produce a site and use any of its proprietary features, the site will only work properly if your account with the host is set up to operate with the FrontPage extensions. The extensions are not required for a straightforward site produced using FrontPage, but they are required for any of its clever features, and this includes practically any form of interaction with users for example. If you build a site using FrontPage it is probably worthwhile using a web host that provides full support for sites built using this program. If you should inadvertently use one of its own special features the site will still work properly. Such is the popularity of FrontPage that even some free web hosting companies now support its extensions.

If you opted for FrontPage support when opening the account for your web space, but with the site uploaded the clever features fail to work, check with the hosting company to see if the extensions have actually been enabled. They should really be installed by default if you opted for them when setting up the account, but mistakes can occur. A web host should have some sort of customer support on their site, or perhaps a helpline or Email support. The customer support service should be able to quickly sort out any problems with FrontPage extensions that fail to materialise.

Filenames

As already pointed out, your site is quite likely to be hosted on a server that runs under UNIX or Linux. In Windows the filename myboat.jpg is effectively the same as the filenames MYBOAT.JPG and Myboat.Jpg. The same is not true with UNIX and Linux where these would be considered as three different names. The practical consequence of this is that it is essential to be consistent with filenames, and to regard them as case sensitive, even though they are not when on your PC. The safest approach is to have all the filenames entirely in lower case letters. If a mistake should be made and an upper case letter slips in somewhere, it is easy to spot and rectify the mistake.

In a similar vein, spaces and unusual characters can cause problems. The case sensitivity problem is limited to UNIX and Linux based web hosting, but the problem with non-alphanumeric characters can also occur with Windows web hosting. The problem is apparently more to do with the way browsers interpret things than with the web hosting. Anyway, it is definitely advisable to avoid anything other than letters and numbers in the filenames of pages, images, etc.

When faultfinding a site it pays to bear in mind that the site will work properly if the correct links are present and the files are also present and in the right place. The majority of problems are caused by files that have not been uploaded at all and by links to the wrong file. Get everything in the right place and correct any links and the site will probably work perfectly.

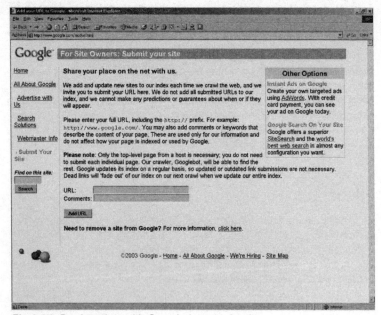

Fig.6.25 Registration with Google is very simple

What site?

Many people seem to think that you simply have to place a site on the Internet and thousands of users will then log onto it every day. I suppose that this could eventually happen provided the web site was up to a high enough standard, but it takes time to build up a large amount of traffic to your site and there is no guarantee that it will ever happen. Your site can be accessed by millions of users, but only a tiny percentage of them will wish to access it, and the rest can only visit the site if they know it is there. There are steps that can be taken to entice as many visitors to your site as possible, if you really have a need for visitors to your site. Most family and personal sites are set up for the benefit of the site creator's family and friends. Visitors might actually be excluded rather than encouraged.

The situation is different with something like a small business or hobby site, which is a bit pointless unless it receives a reasonable number of visitors. Search engines are one of the most important means of getting visitors to your site. Some people are of the opinion that a site may as well not exist unless it is in the databases of a few popular search engines.

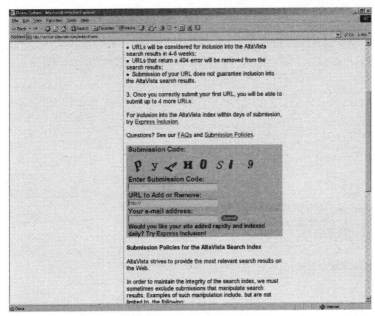

Fig.6.26 Registration with AltaVista is also straightforward

This is probably overstating the case, but if you are not going to advertise your site on the Internet or elsewhere, it is likely that a high percentage of visitors will enter the site via a search engine. Traffic on the site is almost certain to be light until and unless search engines start directing people to it.

Most search engines have automated systems for surfing the Internet and these are known by such names as spiders, robots, and crawlers. You can simply wait in the hope that these automated systems locate your site and add it to their databases. The more reliable approach is to register your site with some of the more popular search engines. The more search engines you register with the greater the number of hits your site is likely to receive. On the other hand, only a few search engines are used by the vast majority of people. Having registered with the top half dozen or so search engines you rapidly get into the realms of diminishing returns. It is important to get your site noticed by all the really big search engines, but going beyond that could just be a waste of time.

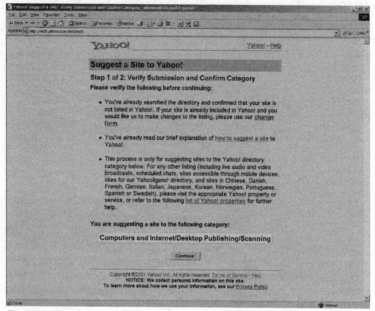

Fig.6.27 The first step when registering with Yahoo!

Google is now by far the most popular search engine and it is also used to provide the results for some major sites, so it is important to register your site with one as soon as possible. The registration process is very simple, and the registration page has two text boxes (Figure 6.25). The address of your site is added into the upper textbox, and a brief comment can optionally be included in the lower one. Note that the address must be the full version such as http://www.babanibooks.com, and not the shortened version such as www.babanibooks.com. Having added the necessary information it is just a matter of operating the Add URL button to register the site. It is only necessary to register the homepage, because the Google crawler should locate the rest. Note that there is no guarantee that Google will include a submitted site in their index, and even when they do add the site it can be a while before it finally goes into the index.

Matters are nearly as straightforward with AltaVista (Figure 6.26). The code in the box above the textboxes has to be entered in the relevant field, and this is presumably done to prevent automated systems from bombarding AltaVista with registration requests. The full URL of your site and your Email address are added in the other two fields of the form.

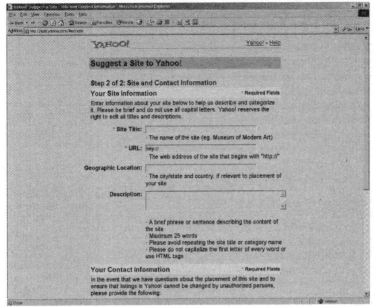

Fig.6.28 Site details, etc., are added using this page

Operate the Submit button when all the information has been entered. As with Google, there is no guarantee that your site will make it into the index, or that it will stay there if you are successful. Also, it could be some while before your information is processed.

Yahoo!

Yahoo! does things differently, and there is no submission page as such. However, you can suggest a site, including your own, by first going into the section of Yahoo!'s directory that is most relevant to your site. Somewhere on the page, and usually at the bottom or near the top right-hand corner, there will be a Suggest a Site link. Activating this link produces a page where you have a choice of paying for an entry into the directory or submitting the site free of charge. Selecting the free option brings up a page like the one in Figure 6.27. This gives some general information about submitting a site to Yahoo!, and it also asks you to ensure that the site is not already in the directory. There is no harm in doing so, but if you completed the site an hour or two earlier there is no

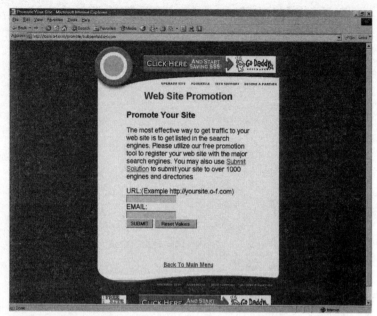

Fig.6.29 Some web hosts have a facility for registering with several search engines at once

chance of it already being there. Operating the Continue button brings up the page of Figure 6.28, and this is where details of the site are entered. Only the site's title, its full URL, and the contact information are required fields. Operate the Submit button to complete the process.

Many web space providers make life easier for their customers by providing a utility that enables a site to be simultaneously submitted to a large number of searches engines and Internet directories. This is sometimes in the form of a program that is run on your PC, but these days it usually a web page where you fill in the URL and your Email address and press the submit button. Figure 6.29 shows the site promotion page of www.o-f.com If your web host provides a good and free feature of this type then it probably a good idea to use it. Some of these services are free if you will settle for a cut-down version, but require a fee to be paid if you need the full service. There are a number of web sites that offer this type of deal. It might be better to manually submit your site to a select-few search engines rather than use a cut-down service.

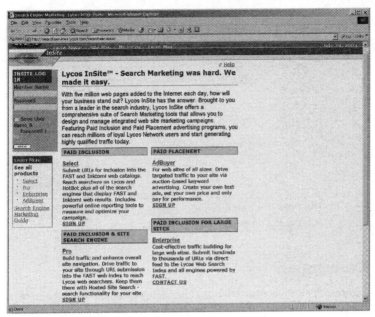

Fig.6.30 Registration is not always free

Paying up

Note that there is sometimes a charge for submitting your site direct to a search engine. Lycos for example, has four options when submitting a site (Figure 6.30), but none of them are free. With most search engines there is the option of paying a fee when submitting a site, and you obviously get an improved service when a fee is paid. You invariably get a faster service as well, and there may be additional benefits such as guaranteed inclusion in the index and a high ranking when your site appears in search results. In the case of Google, you can opt for their Adwords scheme, and your text-only advertisement will then appear alongside or above related search results. Note that most search engines only accept submissions from commercial sites via the paid for route. For a commercial site it is probably worth paying for special treatment by at least a couple of the largest search engines, but the fees involved are probably a bit too high for non-commercial users.

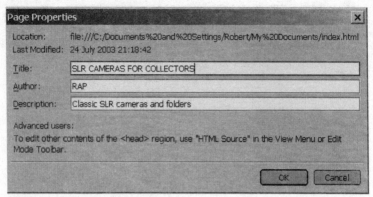

Fig.6.31   The Page Properties window of Netscape Composer gives access to some meta tags

Showing up

Getting your site into the indexes of search engines does not guarantee that your site will turn up in search results, and it certainly does not mean that it will be at the top of the results. It is probably a mistake to design a site to suit search engines rather than users, but there are some points that should nevertheless be borne in mind. Text in the form of an image file will not be picked up by a search engine, and the same is true of any text in photographs. It is possible to make some really nice banner headlines using a graphics program, but the headlines are images and not text, and will be treated as such by the spider of a search engine. A site that has pictures but little or no text is likely to be invisible to the search engine spiders. Some search engines, including Google, take note of Alt text in their web crawls, but some search engines do not.

There are usually several criteria that determine which matches appear at the top of the list, but external links are often given the greatest weighting. External links are important anyway. There are three basic ways of getting people to view your site, which are advertising, search engines, and links from other sites. Non-commercial sites are not normally promoted by advertising, which leaves just links and search engines. Some good links will probably match or exceed the number of visitors brought in by search engines. Reciprocal links with sites of a similar nature will help to bring visitors to your site and will move all the linked sites higher in the search engine results.

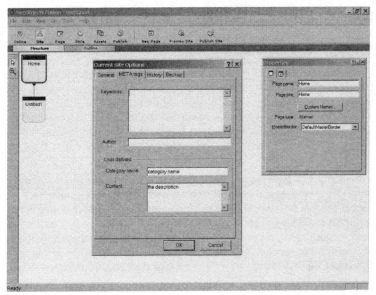

Fig.6.32   In Fusion the Current Site Options window has a section for meta tags

The text in your site should already contain words that are likely to match with the search strings used by people looking for a site of that type. It does no harm to read through the text to make sure that there are no glaring omissions. Descriptive page titles that contain likely search words should help. Witty subheadings that are clever plays on words might be funny, but they could simply confuse visitors quickly scanning your site. They could be even more confusing to search engines. Pages that use simple and straightforward HTML are generally considered to be more search engine-friendly than pages that use complex HTML, where the spider may never get as far as your text. Sites that use frames can give the spiders problems, but this will not usually be a problem these days.

Most search engines make some use the description meta tag, and where possible it is advisable to make sure that this contains a brief and valid description of the site. Unlike the title meta tag, the contents of which provide the text in the title bar of the browser, the contents of the description meta tag are not seen by users of the site. It should be possible to add meta tags when using a WYSIWYG web creation program, and in Netscape Composer this feature is accessed via the Format menu. Selecting the Title and Page Properties option produces the window of Figure 6.31. The text added into the description field is used as the contents of the description meta tag.

There is a similar facility in Fusion (Fig.6.32) that is accessed via the Tools menu. Select Options and then Current Site, and then operate the META Tags tab in the window that appears. No description field is included but there is one for keywords. In theory this can be used to add words that do not appear on the page but could aid searches. Unfortunately, most search engines now ignore any information here, so adding keywords might have a limited effect.

Ultimately, the best way to get visitors to your site is to make it really interesting and useful with everything well laid out and presented. A good site will always shine through and attract visitors. No amount of promotion will bring a continuous stream of visitors to a poor or indifferent site. Unfortunately, if your site is about an obscure and unpopular subject it is unlikely to receive large numbers of visitors however good it is, and however well it is promoted. Try to be realistic about your expectations.

Registration URLs

Google   http://www.google.com/addurl.html

AltaVista   http://addurl.altavista.com/addurl/new

Lycos   http://searchservices.lycos.com/searchservices/

Alltheweb   http://www.alltheweb.com/add_url.php

Yahoo! information http://docs.yahoo.com/info/suggest/

Points to remember

Many web page creation programs have a built-in facility for uploading sites. Where a facility of this type is available it will almost certainly represent the easiest way of uploading sites. The capability for maintaining sites might be limited though.

An FTP program can be used to upload and download sites, upload an additional page, rename a page, etc. This gives full control over the site making it easy to keep it up-to-date, but it is also possible to make a complete mess of things unless you are careful. WS-FTP LE is a useful FTP program that is available as a free download.

Most web space providers now have so-called browser uploading facilities. Either a "clever" web page or an applet is used to enable files to be uploaded, renamed, deleted, etc., using an ordinary browser. These are generally easier to use than an FTP program.

There are many millions of Internet users, but there are also many millions of sites. Simply placing a site on the Internet does not guarantee large numbers of visitors will flock to the site. People can only visit the site if they know it is there, and its URL.

It is important to submit your site to at least a few of the large search engines if you wish to attract substantial numbers of visitors. Most search engine companies allow non-commercial sites to be submitted free of charge. There is often a charge for registering commercial sites, but there should be benefits such as guaranteed inclusion and a higher rating in the results.

Design your site to suit users rather than the spiders of search engines, but make sure that the text in your pages includes the words that people are likely to use in search strings when looking for a site such as yours. Remember that any text in an image file will not be detected by the search engine.

Having reciprocal links with other sites will help to bring visitors to your site. It will also help to get your site, and the linked sites, higher in search engine results. Promoting your site will be a waste of time unless it has good quality content that is well presented. Produce a really good and interesting site and it should eventually triumph.

Index

A

add-ons 127
Adobe Acrobat 15
Adobe PDF 74
Aif or Aiff 14
album 136, 270
album page 145
aligning objects 131
alignment 229, 234
Alt text 100
AltaVista 296
anchors 37, 235
applet 115, 288
artefacts 160
artistic filters 186
aspect ratio 144, 168
AVI 15

B

background 21, 60, 126
background colour 9, 248
background image 180, 248
bandwidth 89
banner 88
Baseline compression 171
bitmap 12, 158, 195
Blend effect 128
blur filtering 195
body tag 9
bold 119
bounding box 252
brightness 180, 187
browser 104
browser safe 188
browser upload 288
bulleted 237
button 30, 65

C

camera 151
caption 100, 209

case sensitive 293
cell 24
cells 211
CGI 18
clipart 117
code 220
Color Picker 185
colour 9, 59
colour (linked text) 123
colour scheme 61
colour-blind 61
column 24
Composer 222
compression 157, 170
configuration window 283
consistent approach 61
content 218, 246
content frame 27
contrast 180, 187
contrasting colours 60
controlling compression 170
controls 180
Copy and Paste 129, 229
copyright 5
Counter object 128
crawlers 295
Crop tool 162
cropped 153
cropping 144, 160
CSS 17
cursor 211, 237

D

databases 295
design 55
DHTML 16
Diamond gradient 183
digital camera 151
directory structure 32
DOM 17
dots per inch 156
download 38

download time	70, 172
downtime	89
drop shadow	195
dummy content	218

E

editing	107, 141
enlargement	252
entering text	19
explanatory text	76
export	221
extensions	18, 264
external links	300

F

family site	2
fan sites	5
faultfinding	290
feathering	165
file conversion	191
file management	286
file types	12
FileManager	288
filenames	293
files	40, 133, 203
filters	174, 186
Flash	15
font	6, 62
format	45
frames	26, 65
framesets	28
free web hosting	88
FrontPage	18, 262
FTP	50
FTP access	133
FTP program	96, 280, 282
Fusion	19, 241

G

gallery	254
generating backgrounds	182

Geocities	94
Ghostscript	75
GIF	13, 191
Google	57, 296
Gradient tool	183
graphics	151
guided tour	66

H

handles	209
heading	1, 20, 63, 227
height	234
hired space	92
hobby sites	5
homepage	94, 215
horizontal lines	234
hosting	88
hot spots	35
HTML	6, 133, 199
HTML editor	47, 134
HTML export	221
HTML files	133
hyperlink	8, 64, 200

I

ID	95
image editing	141
image files	44
image size	168
images	69, 152, 209, 249
index.html	278
Indexed Color	188
integral upload	275
interactive	127
Internet connection	70
ISP hosting	91
italic	119

J

JavaScript	16, 288
Jpeg	12, 157

Jpeg compression 158

L

large business site 3
large text 193
limited bandwidth 92
lines 22, 234
link colour 200
link text 121
linking files 40
links 31, 56, 111, 235, 300
Linux 293
lists 22, 76, 227

M

mark-up 8
markers 184
Marquee tool 162
Media Player 43
menus 129
meta tag 301
MIDI 16
minimalism 57
missing FrontPage 292
missing homepage 292
missing material 72
modem 11
monitors 188
Mov 15
MP3 16
Mpeg or Mpg 15
multi-channel site 6
multimedia 44
music 69

N

named anchors 37
navigation buttons 244
navigation frame 27, 247
Navigator 222
Neon filter 145

Netobjects Fusion 241
Netscape Composer 222

O

online business 4
online printing 144
ordered lists 23

P

padding 26
page creation programs 48
PageBuilder 115
PageMaker 7 221
paragraph 19
Paste 68, 120, 229
Pastel filter 145
PCX format 45
PDF 15, 43
PDF995 75
Perl 18
personal site 2
perspective effects 195
photo albums 134, 270
Photo Express 160
photo gallery 254
photo page 98
Photoshop 7 161
Photoshop Elements 2 161
physical size 167
picture quality 157
pictures 203
pixels 151
Png 13, 192
pop-ups 71
preview 103
promotion 275
public domain 5
publishing 280

Q

QuickTime 15

Index

R

rasterizing	195
register	296
registration URLs	302
relative links	31
resize	168
resolution	137, 152
robots	295
rollover	121, 155
roundtrip HTML	7
row	24

S

scanners	151
screen resolution	62, 156
scrollbars	30, 141
search engines	295
server	89
Sharpen filter	174
Sharpen More	176
site map	244
small business site	2
software	45, 199
spacing	26
spelling checker	74
spiders	295
Standard compression	171
style	74, 246
subdomain	92
subfolder	32, 203
subheadings	1, 76
substitute font	62
support files	203
swatches	123
Swf	15

T

tables	23, 209, 225
tags	9, 11, 301
template	207
testing	256

text	118, 193
text colour	21, 119
text cursor	211
text size	62
text styles	119
theme	57
thumbnail	70, 138, 256
tiled background	181
Time and Date	128
title bar	242
Txt	14

U

under construction	77
underline	119
UNIX	293
unordered	23, 237
Unsharp Mask	177
uploading	50, 96, 275
URL	64, 292

W

Warp Text	195
web graphics	151
web hosting	88, 94
web publishing	87, 96
web site templates	265
wizard	80, 241
WMA and WMV	16
Word	73, 200
word processor	120, 199
worst of the web	56
wrapping	231
WS_FTP LE	282
WYSIWYG	7, 48, 115, 224

X

XML	17

Y

Yahoo!	94, 297